Praise for *Gutsy*

"Without boldness, you can't live the life you want. *Gutsy* is a fresh perspective on ways to live the happiest, boldest, most self-loving, and compassionate life we all deserve."

—Emma Seppälä, PhD, author of
The Happiness Track and science director of
the Stanford University Center for Compassion
and Altruism Research and Education

"Dr. Leah Katz beautifully weaves together her experience as a psychologist, the practice of mindfulness, and her own life story to help those feeling stuck and wanting to create forward movement in their lives."

—Natalie Jill, author of *Natalie Jill's 7-Day Jump Start*

"*Gutsy* is relatable, smart, and filled with real tools for how to work through anxiety and use mindfulness to show up as your most authentic self. Katz has a unique way of making mindfulness cool and approachable, so readers actually want to take tools from this book and make real change in their lives. I know this book will help so many."

—Amanda E. White, LPC, author of *Not Drinking Tonight* and creator of @therapyforwomen

"Leah Katz has nailed what it takes to be *gutsy* from the inside out. Katz tackles core elements of what it means to be human, offering both personal and research-based paths for exploration and transformation. *Gutsy* is set against the backdrop of Katz's personal journey of self-discovery and healing, offering potent vignettes that enliven the process of cultivating 'gutsiness.' This book is a love letter to women finding their way to themselves. If you are drawn to this book, trust it!"

—Jennifer Nurick, clinical psychotherapist,
energetic healer, founder of Psychotherapy Central,
and president of the International Energetic Healing Association

"Dr. Leah Katz delivers a refreshing look at mindfulness, and she does so not only from her broad clinical expertise but through her own experience and vulnerability. This book is enlightening, entertaining, and brave. It's also, as the title suggests, *gutsy*."

—Lair Torrent, LMFT, author of *The Practice of Love: Break Old Patterns, Rebuild Trust, and Create a Connection That Lasts*

"Leah Katz provides a refreshing and accessible take on incorporating mindful practice to enhance our well-being and take us a step closer to inner congruence. As someone who believes in the value of enhancing our metacognitive awareness, I will be recommending this book to both clients and loved ones as a valuable tool to aid this endeavor."

—Joshua Fletcher (@anxietyjosh), psychotherapist and author

"Katz brings us along on her journey of overcoming fear in the face of living life to the fullest and empowers the reader with mindful questions and exercises. This work is a wonderful addition to anyone's path of healing and self-reflection."

—Matthias Barker, psychotherapist and author of *On Avoiding Burnout*

"In our distracted world, Dr. Katz demystifies mindfulness so that it becomes a practical pathway to living your truest, fullest, most present life. Who doesn't need that? This book truly is for everyone."

—Niro Feliciano, LCSW, psychotherapist and author of *This Book Won't Make You Happy*

"Katz's book skillfully interweaves anecdote with advice, both tactical and philosophical, and reclaims the notion of *gutsy* as an inside job. It's about the small, daily moves that bring us closer to our center, not the flashy ones that draw a crowd. A wonderful reminder that living big is about the incremental, consistent moves we make along the way."

—Brie Doyle, author of *You Should Leave Now*

Gutsy

Mindfulness Practices for Everyday Bravery

Leah Katz, PhD

Broadleaf Books
Minneapolis

GUTSY
Mindfulness Practices for Everyday Bravery

Cover image: Qweek/iStock
Cover design: Laura Drew

Print ISBN: 978-1-5064-8164-7
eBook ISBN: 978-1-5064-8165-4

Contents

Introduction

I was at a women's retreat several years ago where each of the participants were asked to choose a name for themselves for the weekend. There were names like Happy Hearth, Tall Tree, Flowing River (you get the idea). We each had to choose something to put on our name tags that we thought reflected who we were in some way and that we would be called for the next three days. I decided not to overthink the name I chose and went with one that felt like a nice representation of myself: Quiet Fire.

Quiet Fire felt like a good fit at the time, and I've found myself coming back to these two words thrown together in the few years since this retreat. There is something profound and deep to me about this combination. To me, the name Quiet Fire embodies what *gutsiness* means: it's a quality of how we approach life that is not big, splashy, ego based, or in your face. No. It's *stronger* than that—and subtler. Gutsiness and bravery are solid and growing forces. But they are often quiet. And gentle. So much so that they are easily missed much of the time. They are kind and full of compassion (for the self and others) and driven by self-awareness and authenticity—and discipline and courage. They are deeply personal and empowering.

I think if we pause, right now even, and get quiet with ourselves, we can all identify the quiet fire that burns within us—even those of us who don't know that it is there, or deny it, or think it's silly, or are frightened by it. This quiet fire is what keeps us from complacency and keeps us instead wanting more for ourselves and our children. Even if we find ourselves in a spot where it is hard to put those yearnings into practice, our quiet fire is the soul-stirring feeling we get from wanting to live and build our most meaningful lives. It's an inner sense, hard to articulate and difficult to put into words. It's wisdom and inner strength and the desire to shake things up.

In this book, we will discuss practical strategies to put those qualities of inner strength and confidence into motion while we build and reinforce the awareness of the truth that we are all strong and brave, whether we acknowledge it or not. Growing from that truth, acknowledging the fire, and letting it continue to burn slowly, steadily, and strongly are what being gutsy means.

When was the last time you thought of yourself as being gutsy?

If you're like so many of us, the answer is probably not that recently or that frequently.

What if you could change your frame of mind to realize that not only *have* you been gutsy, but you are also making a series of brave and gutsy choices all the time, every day?

In Western society, we use the word *brave* in so many different contexts but mostly in reference to someone doing something extraordinary and beyond human capacity. Think of a Liam Neeson or a Tom Cruise character or Jason Bourne in one of his many movies doing (and surviving!) the unthinkable to seek justice or save someone's life. Often, we think of bravery as an act of explicit courage where someone does something truly remarkable and earth-shattering.

But these are not the only appropriate usages of the word *brave.*

Similarly, the word *gutsy* evokes at times doing something with chutzpah, or brazenly. It suggests doing something not sanctioned by society. It can sometimes be associated with reckless, unskillful, or insensitive behavior. *Gutsy,* in this book, is defined as an offshoot of bravery. It's the muscle we use when we choose to do something against the grain, outside of society's expectations of us. It's when we sit and meditate and let ourselves really *feel.* We are gutsy in the moments where we find ourselves staring at two options. Option one is the same old choice, leading me down the same old path of feeling stuck, jealous, angry, powerless, or resentful. Option two is where we take a deep breath and choose another path for ourselves, one that is hard and scary to forge but also full of hope and excitement and possibility. This path is brave, true, and reflective of our inner wisdom and knowing of ourselves. It is the one that, at the end of the day, is self-determined.

A lot happens that is beyond our control in life. We often show up for other people in ways that are hard, but we do it for the sake of responsibility and compassion. Being gutsy is building the self-awareness to know where and when to create boundaries, when we choose to intentionally do things because it is our obligation, and how we choose to respond to the things that are beyond our control. Because, after all, we have one (short) life to live—we want the choices we make to be in line with our values and not driven by unhelpful forces like comparisons, shame, or unprocessed old pain.

Being gutsy is in the big choices: the decision to make a career switch, leave a toxic relationship, or forge a different spiritual path for yourself than what was set out for you by your family. But—and listen up, because this is important and this is the crux of this book—being gutsy is often found in the small choices, the ones that make up the daily fabric of our lives. It's in speaking up for yourself when a boundary has been crossed, getting more authentic and vulnerable with your friends, or complimenting a stranger on their shoes. We find our guts in the everyday moments of showing up. In the small, tiny moments that don't seem like big deals but, when added up, define our lives.

In this book, we define *bravery* as something different from the glamorization of Hollywood and society. It is something you and I are practicing daily.

Though it is rare to hear the more mundane aspects of life lauded as being brave, I believe bravery is something present and woven into the day-to-day fabric of each of our lives.

Each one of us, in this very moment, has more guts than we even know. This gutsiness is the sum total of life's big and small choices that we are faced with every single day. And every single day we are given many opportunities to *lean in* to our experience and practice bravery.

Bravery is found in tough parenting moments and in taking ownership of our fallacies in relationships and really apologizing. It is speaking up when it is hard to do so and when you are afraid of the consequences. It is going to a mother's group in the hopes of making a friend or asking someone new out for a coffee date. It is spending time alone—if being lonely is scary for you—or attending an event despite the anxiety involved. It is seeking therapy or help from another person when your burden feels too heavy for just you. It is speaking out loud your years-old dream to your friends.

It is every single time you choose to pay attention to an uncomfortable thought or sensation, instead of avoiding it.

I guarantee you, without even knowing you or the specifics of your life, that your life so far is an aggregate of plentitudes of brave choices and actions.

> **"Bravery is having the courage to show up and face our fears."**

Bravery is having the courage to show up and face our fears. Sometimes this means staying with something that is difficult, paying attention to the areas of difficulty, and finding a way to work through it. Sometimes this means making a difficult choice and leaving a situation that is no longer working for you.

But whatever way you spin it, *bravery* and *gutsiness* mean taking an honest look at what is going on in your life and facing it. Showing up for the hard stuff, doing the hard thing, whatever that means to you. And practicing bravery is not relegated to outward actions or easily definable moments or behaviors. It is often something more subtle, internal, and solitary.

Being brave means being unafraid of the thoughts, feelings, and external and internal judgments that are a part of our everyday lives. We all have ugly and uncomfortable thoughts and feelings we'd rather not have, some more conscious than others. These mental events and psychological states can certainly be painful. However, when we don't talk about them and pretend they don't exist, we run into suffering.

We lead with bravery when we take an honest look at what is going on inside. Sometimes there is an actionable behavior that flows from that awareness.

But there isn't always a way of measuring bravery.

In my clinical practice and personal life, I have seen too many people, of all ages, tell themselves a story of how *unbrave* they are.

Feeling *unbrave* is exactly as it sounds: not accessing and allowing your bravery to shine through and believing your mind's story that you don't have what it takes to do what it is that your innermost wisdom and yearnings would have you do.

At the same time, in my clinical practice, I have been struck over and over again by the bravery my clients have displayed in our work together. Young, middle-aged, or older clients—being brave is independent of age. I am not trying to minimize the tremendous work it often takes to be brave. Being brave, being gutsy, can be difficult, but it is not insurmountable. Often, learning to be brave can be aided through supports we put into place: therapy, close friends, reflective exercises, and so on.

Let's be *brave*. Let's live our fullest, truest lives.

Humans have a fathomless capacity to be brave. If we let ourselves access that innate bravery, we can open up the doors to a life that is truer and fuller. Being brave can lead to greater depths of spirituality, confidence, and well-being.

Practicing mindfulness—the exercise of kindly paying attention to the present moment, over and over again, one moment at a time—can be one conduit to bravery. Studies have shown the dual relationship between bravery and mindfulness: it takes guts to practice mindfulness, to face the hard stuff with a gentle awareness; and in turn, in practicing mindfulness, we increase our opportunity to be gutsy.[1]

I have found this to be true in my own journey with practicing mindful meditation. Learning to slow down and show up to what my mind was producing was the biggest catalyst in helping me access my own bravery. I began seriously meditating over seven years ago; although I had espoused meditation for a long time before then, I hadn't had very much experience with my own formal practice.

It was almost happenstance how I ended up on my first meditation retreat (more on that later), and something I am forever grateful for. Since then, I have gone on other retreats and maintain my own formal and informal practice. I find the practice of meditating nurturing, a way of checking in with myself and carving out stillness in my increasingly busy life. It often feels like getting a massage for my soul.

Don't get me wrong, though: it is not always a pleasant experience. Sometimes it can feel quite wily.

The powerful lessons I have learned through my own practice of mindfulness are ones I try to weave into the clinical work I do with teenagers and adults, hoping to impart the power of creating a gentle awareness of our mind's storytelling and the brave choices we can then make. I aim to communicate that we are not wedded to anything our mind produces.

Similarly, as mentioned above, therapy can be an important conduit to address deeply held beliefs, stories, and fears that hold us back from living a profoundly rewarding life. We don't have to be in crisis to go for therapy. It can provide support in so many different ways including insight and skill building. I am constantly awed and inspired by the privilege of getting down and dirty, so to speak, with my clients and watching them show up for themselves and create change.

This showing up is reflected in coming to a therapy session (which can be very difficult, as some of you may know) and flowers when the client chooses to talk about and face life's most uncomfortable sensations and realities. The bravery I witness continues as the people I work with make active, challenging choices to shift their relationship to whatever is causing them pain.

I am inspired daily working with my clients, watching them learn and grow and grapple with the stuff most of us are compelled to avoid. Mindfulness and my experience with my own therapy have put me on a path where I am committed to working through old trauma, developing a strong relationship with the person I am today (and watching with loving curiosity as I evolve!), and making brave, wise choices to move forward. Did you know that a study out of Germany found that people in therapy show better outcomes when their therapist has trained in Zen meditation?[2] Though this evidence is not conclusive by any means, it points to the power of acceptance. Working with a therapist who has trained in the art of being present—in a nonjudgmental way—helps the client heal.

In this book, we'll delve into the more intimate personal aspect of what is holding us back from living an awakened life—because we cannot reach our dreams, or even know what they are, if we don't first attend to sources of pain within us. We all carry pain. It is a part of life. It is an integral part of our story. How we choose to approach our unique pain can define our ability to pursue and actualize our dreams.

This book contains ideas that I hope will help you navigate the difficult aspects of life, which we all share to some degree. My hope for you, and me, and all of us is that we access enough insight, guts, and wisdom to meet the brave, wise self that is already inside.

We will talk about destructive narratives that may be holding us back and move into building up a healthier narrative and behavioral repertoire that ultimately will open the door for brave, wise choices that can lead to a more meaningful and spiritual existence.

We will build ourselves from the ground up, so to speak.

This book is from my heart to yours. It is comforting and joyful for me to imagine you in your own little corner of this world creating space in your oh-so-busy life to read this. It is inspiring to think of you carving out time for yourself and going forth into your life feeling more empowered to live your life to its fullest.

For you moms who wake up early in the mornings and put on your cozy robe to drink your cup of coffee, who sneak away for a few minutes of the day to practice gratitude, or meditation, or whatever you hold in your personal space.

For you beautiful people who dream of setting some precious time aside just for you but are having a hard time making it happen because you are just so tired, and who, when it comes down to it, need to stay in bed a little longer because it was a rough night with the kids.

For you who struggle with doubt and insecurity but who have also had great achievements and successes that you don't attend to or celebrate enough.

For you who may have lost track of your own inner worthiness and greatness, feeling like it is inaccessible even though it is merely covered up with other stuff.

For you who walk my walk and understand this language of balancing parenthood and life's responsibilities with personal growth and accomplishment.

This book is for you.

Author's Note

Mindfulness has been defined by Jon Kabat-Zinn as "paying attention in a particular way: on purpose, in the present moment, and nonjudgmentally."[3] The form of meditation that I practice is centered on these principles, and many of the ideas found in in this book originated from insights I have learned through my own practice of meditation.

The concept of mindfulness has become quite popular these last several years. And people are using the word *mindfulness* to imply many different things. The mindfulness I am referring to is that which is cultivated through deliberately paying attention to our experience of any given moment—through our breathing, our body, or a particular sensation—in a kind and nonjudgmental way.

The practice of mindfulness is scientifically linked to many positive outcomes, such as learning to live with uncertainty, making fewer mistakes, being brave, and experiencing longevity, among many other things. These correlations may be enough in and of themselves to get you curious about what this concept of mindfulness is really all about.

I want to emphasize that while it is enticing to practice mindfulness with the goal of achieving these outcomes, practicing mindfulness in an outcome-driven way is self-defeating, really. Rather, explore a mindfulness practice with the hope of living a fuller, richer, and braver life, each precious moment to moment.

That said, meditating may not necessarily be for you, and that is okay. Some people have a difficult time with meditation and choose not to pursue a practice, and there is no judgment in that. You don't need a meditation practice to benefit or appreciate this book, which is influenced by lessons learned from mindfulness as well as my training as a psychologist and my own experiences.

***

Two chapters in this book are devoted to learning to live bravely with our bodies—whether we are in a pain-free or a painful state. I want to emphasize here that I am not a medical doctor, and the words in these chapters are not in any way meant to mimic medical advice. My words here are anecdotal in nature only and stem from my experiences with my own body and my own pain and how I have used mindfulness to meet myself with where I am physically at. Always, always follow your doctor's recommendations for caring for your body. Don't do anything suggested in this book that is not right for you. These chapters are meant to get us thinking about—and noticing—the relationship we each have with our own unique body. My hope is that we can all celebrate the miracle of what it means to have a body and learn to be kinder to the one we were given.

***

Several anecdotes about my upbringing are scattered throughout the book. I am calling on the notion of "dual realties" when it comes to those stories: I am telling these stories through my lens with the full recognition that other participants in the events discussed will have their own perspectives and versions of what happened.

It feels important for me to say, from the beginning, that while I discuss some harder elements of my childhood, I know my parents loved me and did the best they could with what they had, and I have great and deep love for them too. This book is *and* isn't about my own unique story. While it contains elements of my own history, I'm only telling my story because I believe there is such a universalness to all of our stories—when we start sharing, we realize how much our stories overlap with each other.

Furthermore, in discussing my experiences with formalized religion, I feel obligated to emphasize that I am writing strictly from my perspective growing up in a little corner of the Orthodox Jewish world. As it is in all religions, there are many variances in religious observance among Orthodox Jews. I know many people who grew up Orthodox, or lived in the Orthodox world for a period of time, who received different messages and experiences than I did.

One of my dear friends who spent many years studying in an Orthodox Jewish all-female seminary in Israel tells me of vastly different experiences, where she felt empowered as a woman to develop a unique and thoughtful relationship to her Judaism. She describes this time in her life as one of intense Torah (Jewish Bible) study, joy, and independence. Please do not take my story as a blanket description of what it looks like to be Orthodox and Jewish.

While I discuss some elements that were harder for me in living a strictly observant life, I don't discuss as much the beauty found within this tight-knit community. There is a huge emphasis on community, support, and being there for others. *Chesed*—acts of kindness—are extraordinarily emphasized and a big part of this way of life. Meal trains for those who are sick or just had a baby are the norm, as are ongoing prayer groups for those who need it and visits to the sick. There is a strong sense of community and a privilege in honoring the blueprint of sages and rabbis and a lineage that is thousands of years old. I don't talk as much about these beautiful elements of this lifestyle, but I do want to mention here, before we get going, that there are profound benefits for those who are in this community that act as a draw for many people who choose to return to their roots, so to speak, and adopt a more observant lifestyle.

***

There are therapeutic stories scattered throughout this book. Please know any identifying information has either been omitted or changed, in order to maintain the anonymity of the people mentioned. So if you think you recognize someone in this book based on descriptive information—you are wrong! It is not them.

Lastly, if you are experiencing mental health difficulties that are interfering with your life, it may be a wise choice to pursue therapy to enable your growth and healing. In the last chapter of this book, I touch on healing from a difficult upbringing. While I am talking about difficulties, this is not meant to replace therapy in any way. I am not addressing people who have severe trauma or abuse in their histories. If you have a history of trauma or abuse, or are struggling with your mental health, seeking therapy may be a good idea. There are many well-qualified and trained professionals to help with creating forward movement for you as well as empowering and helping you to process your history. I recommend seeking your own individual support if that feels right for you. This book is for educational, informational, and anecdotal purposes only and not meant to replace therapy in any way or imply a therapeutic relationship.

Sending you so much love. Happy reading. I hope you enjoy.

Part 1

How long have you been holding on to the idea of making some change in your life, in one way or another and stayed stuck? The thoughts remain background noise, soft chatter, and abstract ideas (or maybe not even that abstract!), not yet realties? This experience, of so badly wanting to *do* something, *start* something, *leave* something (or someone!) but not making it happen are shared by so many.

Many of us either have been there before or are there now, feeling like we want more for our life, or something different, but having a hard time getting there. I know I've felt it and feel it in some ways currently. That's what propelled me to write a book about this topic—the resonance of my own life's experiences, together with witnessing clients feel these very feelings, illuminate to me how common these feelings are.

Feeling stuck is difficult and can lead to feelings of hopelessness, can be deenergizing and exhausting, and can just suck much joy out of life. On the flip side, there is nothing quite like the feeling of getting "unstuck"—taking some tiny action that helps you remember that, indeed rarely, are we objectively and actually stuck. Oftentimes, it's taking the small action, creating some movement, that helps us realize *we* are the ones standing in our own way. And I have felt that exhilarated feeling myself in many ways, watching the illusion of "stuckness" come crashing down by the very hands that put that notion there in the first place—mine (the product of thoughts produced by my lovely mind). We must emphasize feeling stuck is a feeling like all other feelings—and not a reality. Very rarely, if ever, are we actually physically "stuck."

While there is a lot we can't control in our external environment, we have all the control and power in how we choose to respond as well as how we structure and set up our lives. Ironically, often times, we can find much of our control with an embracing of how out of control we really are. Learning to live with uncertainty is a powerful force for change, but more on that later.

It is empowering and powerful learning to step into our agency and be brave to do something different, allowing ourselves to move away from stuckness. I have celebrated these victories in my own life and with clients, and it is one reason I love my job as a psychologist so much—I feel deeply grateful to be doing work infused with so much meaning. And I can't think of much more meaning than watching someone learning new tools, accessing their own bravery, and making change that leads to a more fulfilling and authentic life.

How many of you have had thoughts of making change in your life for some time now and struggled to either initiate change or sustain it? I know I have. I know waking up early and starting my day with a workout transforms my day, and I've successfully done this for periods of time but then let it fall away. Or I've had some good ideas lingering in my mind for some time and let them sit there without putting them into practice.

Why do we do this? Have great ideas, know what we want to do (more or less), and then stay there, stuck in our thoughts, allowing our creative ideas to remain just that—ideas? As I like to say in therapy, there is often going to be some *function* in the *dysfunction*. There is a reason we hold on to unhelpful habits—they serve some purpose. Sometimes they are cozy and familiar, keeping us safely and squarely in our comfort zones. Sometimes the function is protecting ourselves from experiencing certain feelings that we have deemed "too big" or "scary"—like disappointment, rejection, fear, or embarrassment. Whatever the reason is, many of us find ourselves at one point or another knowing that we want to make changes, even knowing what we need to do, and then not doing anything to make it happen.

In part 1 of this book, we take the necessary first step to making lasting change in our life: addressing what has been holding us back all this time as well as building up our capacity for self-love and compassion. We can't fully do this work without building on our self-love.

It's actually quite fascinating how we have all kinds of thoughts that hold us back that we may or may not be aware of. When we pause and gently notice what those thoughts are, we hold the key to making change—because now that we have the awareness of the thoughts our mind is producing that are holding us back, we can do something about those tricky little thoughts.

In the following chapters, we'll talk about how we can access greater self-awareness so we can better know and understand the parts of us that are holding on tightly to the familiar and keeping things stagnant so that we can make the changes we are dreaming of and tap into a more rewarding and fulfilling life.

1

Oh, Those Tricky Excuses (and What's beneath Them)

Oh, hello there, [excuse], nice to see you.
Are you coming along for the ride?

I thought for a very long time (too long!) that I needed a "meditation cushion" in my office before I would be able to sit in there and start my writing.

This is not a joke.

And it took me a long time to order the *perfect* meditation cushion.

Writing this down now on paper, it seems so silly. Seriously, what does a meditation cushion even have to do with writing a book? But in my mind, at the time it made perfect sense. I needed my Zen corner set up so that I could meditate before writing; without it, my writing would clearly suffer.

(And while I'm at it, it would be really nice to have another west-facing window in here. Because I love the west view from our house, and when I sit here at my desk only having the one south-facing window, I just feel less inspired. But, yes, a meditation cushion and a west-facing window—*those* are what I need to write this book!)

These excuses manifest in me feeling like I need to set up my physical environment "just so" before I begin to write, but they also take up space with more internal excuses: "I'm not in the right frame of mind to write," or "I didn't sleep well last night, so clearly my writing will suffer today. I should just take a day off."

And so on.

Can you relate to this? Making excuses for yourself that may seem perfectly legitimate from the outside? My meditation cushion might seem like a silly example, but often the excuses that stymie our everyday bravery seem really reasonable. That's why I call them "tricky little suckers."

Tricky is one of my favorite words. I think *tricky* describes the majority of excuses we make for ourselves. They are sneaky little things that make us believe that they hold some veracity, when in fact they are not. They are just thoughts, and one of my favorite mantras for working with difficult thinking is *"Just because we think, it doesn't mean it's true."*

Here were some of *my* tricky little suckers:

> *I'm not in the right mindset to write today.*
> *I didn't get enough sleep last night.*

Do you see how they really are so tricky? It's because they seem highly believable. Reasonable even. And sometimes they serve as legitimate reasons for why we shouldn't pursue something in the moment. But often, they are sneaky little guys that only serve to get in the way of us doing what will bring value and meaning into our lives.

What better way to start my book than with a chapter on all the silly excuses and reasons I've given myself as to why I shouldn't start it?

The excuses provided here are real and mine, and they all revolved around one false belief: why I couldn't/shouldn't sit at my desk in my office and put words to paper.

> *I'm so tired from the day today; I just want to watch something.*
> *Now is not the right time. Tomorrow.*
> *I'm not feeling inspired.*
> *There are other things I need/want/must do.*
> *I am not old enough yet, have not accrued enough experience yet, to make my mark.*
> *Who am I to do this thing I so desperately want to do?*

Do any of these ring a bell?

I have been there; I have said versions of those excuses to myself for years and years. I have been wanting to sit and write a blog since I first started my internship in psychology about *more than ten years ago.* I remember asking my prospective boss during my interview if I could start a blog at the psychology clinic if I were to get hired. And he said yes.

Did I start it? No. I didn't even write one entry.

The same thing happened at my current job at a group clinic. I remember asking if I could start a blog, being told yes, writing one piece shortly thereafter, and then never writing another. And even then, I never handed over that one piece to a supervisor to read before posting it, so it never got posted.

Why? Why do we do this to ourselves? Have dreams and passions that we excuse away?

We all have dreams, ideas, things we want to be doing. Some people make the choice to pursue what is in their heart and jump in. Just like that. But for many others—including myself—we have the dream and then proceed to create reasons why we can't get to it, *not just yet*. Oh, we'll *get* to it, just not right now, because we really need that meditation cushion—and don't forget the west-facing window—before we can sit down and start writing.

Dreams and goals are two keys to a fulfilling life, and that's something we all want. Living true to what is in our heart is something most of us value.

Some Science on Goal Achievement

> "Those people who didn't give up on their goals, and displayed optimism, had fewer symptoms of depression, anxiety, and panic disorders throughout the study period."

Don't just take it from me. The importance of living a life deeply connected to our goals is supported by research. In one fascinating study that spanned eighteen years, researchers found that those people who didn't give up on their goals, and displayed optimism, had fewer symptoms of depression, anxiety, and panic disorders throughout the study period. This suggests that aspiring toward goals helps with our connection to a meaningful and purposeful life and increases well-being.[1]

Goals and dreams are critical, but it is important that our goals are perceived as attainable. In another study, having goals that were viewed as attainable was related to later psychological well-being.[2]

Take home message? Setting goals is important, but let's chunk them down into smaller, more attainable goals.

Some of us may have trouble setting goals because we fear the inevitable feeling of disappointment if we don't reach them.

But one study found that not reaching goals is *not* necessarily the catalyst for depressive or anxious symptoms. Ruminating—getting stuck in a negative thought spiral about the lack of your goal achievement—is what leads to increased psychological distress. These researchers emphasize that setting goals and thereby pursuing a purposeful direction in life increases well-being. However, how we choose to respond to unmet aspirations makes all the difference: self-kindness is imperative—and not beating ourselves up over falling short. We will talk more about the stories we tell ourselves, and how to cultivate adaptive narratives in chapters 3 and 5.[3]

So let's get clear on our goals! Try writing down your end goal, and map out the baby steps you need to take to get there. This is a great strategy for creating a clear vision of where you want to go and how you'll get there as well as incorporating accountability.

And for those of you who have had trouble implementing this tactic in the past, here's a brief cheat sheet on how to practically map out the small steps: First, before you get to the baby steps, it's important you define where you want to go—your end goal. We need to have a vision of our final destination before we map out how to get there; otherwise, we'll start and stop and lose our way. For those of us who learned to drive pre–smartphones, the analogy would be to MapQuesting the directions before you drive to an unknown destination. (Remember that? If you know, you know.) We can't know what our next steps should be if we haven't clarified where we want to go.

Once we've defined our end goal, we can start mapping out the individual steps we'll take to get us there. If you have an idea of landmark points along the way—bigger things you'll need to do—jot them down as well, but most importantly, map out your next few steps. You may want to get really specific here. If you own a planner (I'm a big believer in old-fashioned paper planners), write down what days and how much time you will allocate to each individual step. Then try to stick to your plan. Though it may be counterintuitive, breaking it down in this defined way and specifying when we will do it decreases the overwhelming sensation that often comes from focusing on the big picture. Don't get worried if you are only able to map out the next few small steps. With some goals, we may have more of an idea of what several of our next steps should be (and even then, it often changes!), but sometimes we won't. Life *will* unfold as we live it. Trust that your next steps will become clearer with every step you take.

> "Life *will* unfold as we live it. Trust that your next steps will become clearer with every step you take."

And here's an important reminder: it's okay to fall off the horse. It happens to all of us. That is not what determines our success—but how we respond to falling off makes all the difference. Just be sure to get back on. Don't discard it all because you've had a momentary (or longer) lapse. It's never too late to pick back up and get going (again).

Persistence is so much more important than getting it right the first time. All we can do is start with the information we have right now and use it to plan the next thing we need to do. I like the question *"What's the next thing I need to do?"* The very next thing. Maybe it's go to sleep and get some rest, maybe it's doing some more research so I am clearer on my next steps, maybe it's mapping out my week in my planner, or maybe it's making a phone call.

Once you've created a soft plan for your next few steps, make yourself accountable. Set a deadline. Tell a friend. Accountability helps keep us honest and at it.

Starting on this journey of honoring and manifesting our goals is a combination of planning, discipline, and trust as well as *always* noticing your small successes and movement. That's crucial in pre-

"All big successes are composed of a series of small successes. The smaller wins are everything."

venting burnout and keeping you on your course. All big successes are composed of a series of small successes. The smaller wins are everything.

I also want to emphasize here that it's important to find the balance between mapping and planning *and* letting go of our attachment to the idea that we can control things. It's really quite a paradox—on the one hand, planning our next steps is important in keeping us tethered to our goals and makes them more attainable, and on the other, we need to embrace the reality that we can't control outcomes. Doing this is not only accurate; it's liberating.

Accepting that there is uncertainty in this process and that we really can't control what happens is powerful because it helps us move toward trusting the process *and* ourselves. We won't have all the answers; the next steps might seem unclear, but by trusting that they *will* unfold in exactly the way they are meant to and that we have the resources within us to both "figure things out" as they come *and* deal with setbacks is what leads to taking healthy risks, dealing with setbacks, and, ultimately, having a more fulfilling life.

We are exactly where we need to be, and any monkey wrenches we encounter along the way (as we inevitably will) are not only building strength and grit but are also taking us closer to where we need to go. Ambition and achieving our objectives is a balancing act among setting goals, allowing things to unfold with a sense of compassion for not always knowing what that will look like, and learning to go with (and honoring) your intuition and instinct.

Perhaps you have more than one goal. Unsurprisingly, goal conflict—two or more goals that seem at odds with one another—is shown to produce psychological distress. Try spending some time identifying what you really want to do. Record on a scale of one to ten how important each goal is to you to help clarify what is most important to you, and take it from there. Think about what we said before about mapping out your next steps—the ones that are a priority for you right now—and try to not get distracted by all the other great ideas you are having. Trust that you *will* get to them. We can't do it all, and if we try to, we will either burn out or get so flustered and overwhelmed by all the ideas we have that we won't get started. Trust, me I've been in both places, and neither is productive.[4]

There are other, more creative ways to set ourselves up for success in actualizing our dreams. Sure, it is important to consciously and concretely take the necessary steps to achieve your goals. And then there's the unconscious, subliminal route to success. Studies show that if we are shown messages that are in line with our goals, we are more likely to make choices consistent with pursuing our goals, even on the unconscious level.[5] So creating visuals for yourself that remind you of your goals, and placing them in your line of sight may really help you accomplish what your heart yearns for. In one study, visualizing an end goal served as a significant motivator to finish an assigned task.[6]

One way to create a visual of your goal is by leaving written reminders around your living space. I'm a big fan of sticky notes—I use them to jot down all kinds of helpful messages. I write down positive affirmations ("good things are coming my way"), reasons why I am doing what I am doing (my "why"), and motivational messages to myself ("I can do this!") as well as put up love notes my children have left me ("I Luv yoo Mommy").

Seeing these messages helps me in many different capacities: grounding me before I do something scary (like a big podcast interview) or getting me out of my head when imposter syndrome or self-doubt crops up. Seeing my why reminds me that my purpose and passion rest both within me and beyond me. I have the same sticky note with my why on my refrigerator, my bathroom mirror, and the corner of my computer screen. These little but important reminders help me get out of my head when I am feeling scared or nervous, recognize that what I am wanting to do goes well beyond me and my fears in this moment, and get back into this moment and the next task.

Having a monthly and daily planner is another great way to visualize goals. On most weeks, I plan out what I want to get done that week, and at the beginning of the month, I create monthly goals. I start most days with a list of five gratitudes and what I want to accomplish that day. It's helpful before each week to write down what I plan on doing on which day so I am more efficient. Writing objectives down in this way is helpful in keeping me on task and creating a flow and continuity of goals. With every new month, I glance back to last month's goals and build off them or add them to the current month's new goal list if I haven't gotten to it yet.

For those of us who lean toward perfectionism, and often feel as if we are never doing enough or as quickly as we want to, writing small and big goals down has the added benefit of keeping a physical log of all that we *are* doing, and creating space for those important feelings of pride and accomplishment. Make sure in your review of what you need to do, you are spending just as much time reviewing and celebrating all that you have already done. Please don't minimize that.

> "When we really listen to our wisdom—our inner yearnings—get out of our heads, and let our hearts dictate where we need to go, we discover timeless truths."

I also keep my old and current vision boards in my line of sight in my home work space. It reminds me of what is important to me. And it is amazing how consistent these old vision boards are with my current dreams. Because when we really listen to our wisdom—our inner yearnings—get out of our heads, and let our hearts dictate where we need to go, we discover timeless truths.

The Role of Fear

We know that our excuses interfere with our ability to live our best lives. But what's behind these reasons and excuses? Why do we put these roadblocks that stop us from starting down a magical and fulfilling journey in *our own way*?

I believe that the answer for many of us is fear.

We all have different fears. For me, a big one is the fear of failure. *What if what I write sounds dumb to other people? What if my writing is immature and unsophisticated? What if my high school English teacher was right, and I'm only a B-level writer? What if what I write offends my family?*

Be careful what you choose to do with these fears. They can easily be the stream of consciousness that dictates your life choices.

Pause here for a moment as you consider the reasons you've given yourself for not pursuing something or other. Be still and notice what comes up.

I love the analogy of an iceberg to illustrate the process of more fully understanding what might be motivating a thought/feeling/behavior. We see just the tip of the iceberg sticking out of the water, and underneath the surface is a huge ice mountain, much larger than what we see above the water. This is similar to our excuses. We tell ourselves reasons why we can't pursue our dreams (like my missing-in-action meditation cushion), but these are the tip of the iceberg, the parts that we can easily see. But what is it really all about? That is the fear, the thoughts beneath the avoidance, the real reasons you have been distracted and not paid attention. That is the part of the iceberg underneath the water.

What are your reasons (the tip of the iceberg) and fears (the mountain underneath) you give yourself for not doing The Thing(s)?

What emotions are coming up as you ponder this question? Sit with these too. Emotions give us information about what is important to us. Is this bringing up some sadness? That's okay! Listen to it! What's behind that sadness? It likely means this Thing means a lot to you.

Other excuses disguised as rational reasoning are self-doubt and—the black widow of excuses—shame. Thoughts such as, *Who am I to put something out there? There are people older, wiser, smarter than me who are better equipped to say things to the public. Will I be any good?*

> "The *tricky* thing with these thoughts, which are rooted in self-doubt, fear, and shame, is that we will never know what we are capable of and what is possible for us unless we try."

The *tricky* thing with these thoughts, which are rooted in self-doubt, fear, and shame, is that we will never know what we are capable of and what is possible for us unless we try. And actually, one of the very best ways to overcome fear is through compassionate exposure: facing that which we fear (in a way that feels manageable and kind). And that's a well-studied fact. It's something I work with almost daily in my clinical work.

The first step in overcoming our fears is to acknowledge them. And that takes bravery. And gutsiness. When we are aware of our negative thinking and limiting thoughts, we can then choose to let go of the thoughts that interfere with brave behaviors. If we are unaware of our thinking, we can be caught in a trap without even realizing it. Being mindful is associated with the trait of bravery.[7]

Often, in therapy when I am with a client, I think of a mound of clay being a good analogy for a "raw" thought. When we acknowledge a thought, it's like we've been given a mound of clay. We get to shape the thought and decide what we will do with it. It doesn't just have to stay a shapeless mound. It can take any form, and the power to do that comes first from an awareness *of* the thought and then from what we choose to do with it. So let's not carry around our fears like heavy ill-defined pieces of clay. Let's set them on the table, take a good look at them, and then mold them into thoughts that better serve us and support us in our journey toward meaning and fulfillment.

(Perceived) Failure

It's going to happen, if you're lucky. Someone won't like you. Something will go wrong. You will not succeed. (This sounds like some sort of anti-pep-talk talk.)

What? Did I just say "lucky"?

Yes. Actually—and I tell this to several of my clients who tend to be perfectionists (like me)—having someone just not like you (or any other form of perceived rejection or failure), with no reason or explanation, can be one of life's greatest gifts and opportunities for growth. It gives us an opportunity to flex the bravery muscle. Because it forces us to come to terms with ourselves, and if processed in a mindful way, helps us learn the priceless lesson that our self-worth is untouchable. No perceived success—or failure—can touch our innate worthiness.

It can also help us take ourselves less seriously. Maybe even learn to laugh at our shortcomings or those persistent and penetrating themes that our mind produces that often hold us back.

For me, professional rejection can manifest in a patient wanting to switch therapists because they feel like I'm not the right fit or they aren't making enough progress with me. Or a parent pulling their child from therapy without telling me why. Sometimes, I just don't know the reason.

Or maybe it's losing sight of my goals, of falling off the goal train and having a hard time getting back on. Or dealing with painful rejections in my personal relationships. Or being told by my child that I am, without a doubt, "the worst mommy ever!" (Oh, good. Not just me?)

Opening yourself up to the possibility of rejection and failure is an essential part of pursuing your dreams.

"Opening yourself up to the possibility of rejection and failure is an essential part of pursuing your dreams."

I remember a session from very early on in my career, when I was still an intern and working with a complex young adult woman. For one session, she brought in her boyfriend to discuss some issues they were having. I remember being afraid walking into that session, unsure of what would happen.

Well, if I was afraid and worried before the session started, I felt exponentially worse when it was done. The boyfriend was fairly belligerent, vacillating between sitting stoically in his chair, not talking, and lashing out at me. I felt intimidated. They were definitely at least a few years older than me, which felt like a big deal at the time. I'm sure I spent the bulk of the session trying to figure out what was going on and how I should respond to the next verbal assault.

At one point, I remember the boyfriend telling me that he didn't want to talk with me because he felt like he was talking to his younger sister. I felt awful. I'm pretty sure I cried.

I was a new PhD, trying hard to embrace my clinical role, and in that moment, I felt like an inept little girl. That session stayed with me for far longer than it needed to; I allowed that feeling of rejection and failure to eat at me far too much.

Luckily, as part of my training, I had access to some good supervision, during which I was able to talk about my shame surrounding this session and reframe this situation so that it felt like less of a personal wound. I learned that it was okay to have a bad session and to not feel like I needed to know all the answers or hit a home run with every single client. Ultimately, with time and talking it through, I was able to let go of this decentering experience and rediscover my footing as a novice therapist.

This process—accepting my work and myself as is—is something I am mindful of as I do my therapy work today. It is something that even now, much further along in my career than I was at the time of my nightmare session, I need to remind myself of occasionally.

Don't get me wrong. It is not that we need to *want* rejection or create it by setting ourselves up. It hurts when it happens, and that's okay. That's a natural human response. It makes sense and belongs.

But when (perceived) failure comes knocking at our doorstep, our response is what matters. We can get caught up in the vicious cycle of creating excuses, listening to our fears, and practicing avoidance—all of which are simply rooted in thoughts created by our minds—and live immobilized. Or we can put out the welcome mat and greet it as an old friend.

I took my driver's test on my sixteenth birthday and failed miserably. I'm pretty sure I almost got into an accident on the road test, and the instructor had to use his emergency brake (yikes!). It took me a full year before I would take another shot at getting my license—one whole year.

That's a long time. And I'm pretty sure I'm not the only one who feels that as I get older, time (and the passing of it) feels more precious. We don't want our fear of rejection or any other fear to have that kind of hold on our lives.

And how many of us are living with these fears chattering in the background, consciously or subconsciously?

Experiencing some rejection or failure every now and then helps us (hopefully!) realize that our self-worth can't and shouldn't come from anyone outside of ourselves. If it

> "Our self-worth can't and shouldn't come from anyone outside of ourselves."

does, then when we experience rejection, it can feel crushing. Experiencing a balanced amount of rejection or failure creates the conduit for us to learn to lean on ourselves and reinforces that our worth is inherent and internal—something that nothing and no one can diminish.

In the therapy anecdote mentioned previously, I allowed that incident to give me way more tinder for my self-doubt fire than it deserved. In hindsight, it would have felt much better for me to more quickly process that situation in a less personalized way, taking the lessons from it that were helpful and embracing (but not making more of them than I had to) the unnecessary and persisting thoughts of shame and self-flagellation for what they were: tricky thoughts. (It was a good thing I had a supervisor to help me do that at a later point.)

Over the years, I have learned to internalize the message that failure and rejection are inevitabilities of life. I have trained myself to challenge those pesky generalized thoughts and related feelings of not being good enough so they don't take up more room than they need to. I have shifted from globalizing thoughts to harnessing them into more specific and localized responses (most of the time). And those times when I do feel overly bad about a situation that didn't go the way I had hoped, I have become familiarized with this shame response and make space for it until it passes.

Knowing we are not perfect and will make mistakes—in whatever capacity—is one of the greatest gifts we can give ourselves. It is a form of self-compassion. And this awareness helps transform those experiences from potential road blocks to moments of insight and growth.

> "This awareness helps transform those experiences from potential road blocks to moments of insight and growth."

Let's (At)tend to Our Yearnings

We all have thoughts, reasons, and *excuses* we use to explain why we shouldn't or can't pursue some goal or dream. Sometimes these reasons are made up, like mist in our minds, and have no rational basis, and sometimes they sprout from actual real-life experiences (like failing a road test).

Let's spend a few minutes here and understand *your* process. What are your dreams or goals? What yearning is there inside of you that you have silently been ignoring? What in your life have you not paid enough attention to? Is it dealing with a difficult set of circumstances that plagues you frequently or from time to time? Is it finally, finally, not feeling so wedded to a difficult childhood and freeing yourself from the perceived limitations that arise from that experience?

If you have a yearning—*any* kind of yearning—it wasn't placed there by accident. It was placed there because it reflects some wisdom, some truth, buried inside of you. Don't minimize it. It is there for a reason. Write it down. Say it out loud. Take your phone, right now, and record yourself saying it. Now play it back. Again. Acknowledge it. *Accept* it.

> "If you have a yearning—*any* kind of yearning—it wasn't placed there by accident. It was placed there because it reflects some wisdom, some truth, buried inside of you."

Next, return to the very first question in this chapter: What excuses have you made that are interfering with your ability to sit and pursue those dreams, step into your power, or make different life choices?

Now, this is a harder one: What's *behind* those excuses? What are the thoughts you tell yourself that act as barriers to you pursuing a deep and meaningful life? What is it you are telling yourself—perhaps without even realizing it— that reinforces your avoidance of paying attention to That Important Thing?

We all have different interests, yearnings, and passions in our lives that we are not attending to, because we don't feel brave, gutsy, or strong enough. It is completely subjective, different for each person. For some it might mean jump-starting a business, leaving an unfulfilling and stressful job, taking a closer look at our intimate relationships, or paying attention to and treating an underlying mental health issue that has been present for a while and disrupting our life. We lose sight of our bravery with so many thoughts, and by doing this, we lose sight of the things that are truly important to us and make do with living a life that is not as full or rewarding as it can be.

It's like living life always wearing your sunglasses. Sunny or cloudy, night or day, you've got those glasses on. You can see okay most of the time—but think of all the detail and richness you are missing. Or think of a gas tank. Why live life at half empty when you could be riding around with a close-to-full tank? The car still drives with half a tank, sure; you may not notice a difference in the ride with more gas in it, but there *is* a difference.

Think of how much farther you can go with a full tank. You're more likely to reach your destination without driving on fumes.

This is the equivalent of living a life where we are not fully in touch with our strength and wisdom, our hopes and dreams. *And* the things that are holding us back. We can get along okay and may even be able to get by without noticing a decrease in meaning or quality because we have become so good at ignoring the inner yearning and pain. But at some point, it catches up to us. Then we realize that walking around like this is preventing us from reaching our goal: a fully rich, empowered life where we are honoring our truths. When we take those sunglasses off, when we learn to take a good look at our dreams and what reasons our brain has been producing to interfere with what we really want, we can finally live a life of intense color.

Ask yourself these questions:

What is my dream, or area of pain, that needs attention?
What thoughts have my mind produced that are interfering with me accomplishing my dream?
What's underneath these thoughts, the real cause of the excuse?
And now, how can I make space for that fear—but only let it be a part of the bigger picture—so that it doesn't pull me around on a leash?

Now, back to those tricky thoughts that can act like excuses: hold them, honor them, and gently move them next to you, instead of in front of you, so that they don't stop you from doing what you love. Befriend them, embrace them in a warm hug—don't be afraid of them. By doing this you are reminding yourself that you have the power and the strength to accomplish whatever is in your heart. Or at the very least, show up with all you've got and try.

I used these exact strategies to write this book. Remember earlier on in this chapter when I said writing was something I have been wanting to do for forever? Well, here I am doing it. Something just *clicked* for me before my thirty-fifth birthday, and suddenly I *knew* that I just *had* to pay attention to my dreams and yearnings. I couldn't push them off any longer. My long-lasting excuse had been, *I want to write a book, but I have no idea what I should write about, and anyway I'm too young.*

Behind that excuse? Fear of failure.

That excuse stopped being cute a long time ago. I learned to acknowledge it, make space for it when it arises, and set it aside (over and over again), and then I chose to reside in the part of me that is brave by taking the steps to write the book you now hold in your hands.

Once you have identified the underlying reason for your excuse, acknowledge it out loud. Try saying:

Hello, [fear of failure]. You are here right now, and that's okay.
But I'm not going to let you control what I choose to do and not do. I will not make my life's decisions based on you.
I am not going to try to make you go away.
But I am choosing to embrace the entirety of my life, honoring myself, my dreams, and my longings.
If you'd like, you may come along for the ride.

2

Self-Acceptance

Will you take me in as I am?

I remember the moment I read this saying for the first time. I was in my bed in Westchester, New York, several years before I moved to Portland. It was late at night, and I was reading the wonderful book by Steven C. Hayes, *Get Out of Your Mind and Into Your Life: The New Acceptance and Commitment Therapy*, with a pen in my hand, making notes in the margins. This was the first book on ACT (acceptance and commitment therapy) that I had ever read, and it had been recommended to me by my therapist. This workbook completely shifted how I viewed my experience of painful thoughts and feelings, and I have recommended it several times since then.

When I came across *"Will you take me in as I am?"* that evening, I read it and reread it several times. It was a novel concept for me. It was one of those sayings that struck me deep inside. Since that time, I have repeated this saying over to myself countless times, often in a situation where I am feeling anxious. I said it to myself before defending my dissertation, and I have said it when facing a difficult session—both in my own therapy and in my clinical practice. I have said it to myself before asking for a raise at work and on the long walk down the hallway to the waiting room to greet an anticipated tough session. This saying has a way of grounding me, reminding me that it is okay to be just as I am and in whatever circumstance I am in. So long as I have myself (and we will all always have ourselves) and I can hold my space in compassionate awareness, acknowledging where I am with kindness, I will be okay.

Will you take me in as I am?

This is a question that I am not asking someone else. This is a question I am asking *myself.* Can I take myself in as I am, right now, in this very moment? With my nerves, my fears, my imperfections? Because I know somewhere deep inside me that if the answer to that question is no—*No, I cannot be with myself in whatever moment I find myself in, with all that is here for me in my thoughts, feelings, and body*—then I cannot really, truly live my fullest life.

If the answer to this question is a resounding no—*No, I cannot be with myself in this present moment*—then we are judging ourselves, really. We are allowing our fear to guide us and make our decisions. And when we judge ourselves, we're living a life in our heads, focusing too much on our insecurities and fears. The importance of the moment, our ability to be kind observers of our experience, falls away, and we are not present for this one moment, this one life, as it unfolds around us.

Will you take me in as I am?

There is something in these words that leads to confidence. Confidence without needing a reason. Confidence that being you, whoever and wherever you are, is all that you need at this very moment. Confidence to let go of your judgment of yourself. You have what you need to get by. You don't need anyone else's words or experience or looks. In this moment—and, after all, really, in this *life*—all you need is you. This is a lesson in self-reliance. In this moment, all you have and all you need is yourself, with all that you are. You have the inner wisdom, strength, and resilience to live your life. And it doesn't always have to go as planned (as it doesn't). It's a reminder of that too—I am here for this. Whatever this is—a good session, a hard session, things going well for me—or not.

Will you take me in as I am?

This is a message that is helpful for all of us, no matter what life circumstances we find ourselves in.

Can you take yourself in as you are, getting up in the middle of the night with a baby who won't stay asleep for more than a couple of hours? Can you embrace who you are in *this* moment, the you who is full of frustration, exhaustion, and even resentment?

Can you recognize your inner worthiness and fortitude even in moments where you feel much less than a super star?

Can you take yourself in after what you may have perceived as a failure at your job: being turned down for a promotion, making a mistake, getting some negative feedback, having an argument with your significant other? How do you deal with those moments? Can you accept yourself in those moments too and recognize that you are enough?

Can you embrace your insecurities? Your challenges? The feelings of being an imposter that can creep up for so many of us after we've had a success? When you are unsure that you are equipped to face the next moments of your life, can you take yourself in with all of that and choose acceptance?

Will you take me in as I am?

"So long as I can be with myself, in a compassionate and accepting way, I will be good. I will be okay."

In challenging moments, where self-doubt looms over me and is entirely believable, I try to cultivate the voice that reminds me that so long as I can be with myself, in a compassionate and accepting way, I will be good. I will be okay. Even if the meeting doesn't go well and I feel bad about the outcome, as long as I accept myself, I am okay.

The Buddha's famous teaching that "life is suffering" doesn't mean life is meant to be terrible. It alludes to the fact that we humans are primed to get attached to things, and things inevitably change or turn out differently than what we had hoped for. Getting attached to outcomes that either will change or that we have little control over can easily set us up for a life of suffering. If we can recognize our urge to put too much stock in the outcome (even a good outcome), make space for uncertainty and change, and recognize that at the end of the day, all that we really have control over is how we respond and how we love ourselves and connect to ourselves in all the moments, we set ourselves up for a lighter life.

I have echoed these words—*Will you take yourself in as you are?*—in many a session. Some of the people I have spoken to about this felt that it resonated with them. Others did not, and needed other words to carry forth this message into their hearts. And that is okay too. But taking a moment before we have to do something scary, or pausing while in the midst of certain discomfort or pain, and reminding ourselves that we are enough as we are right in this moment can be a grounding way of anchoring ourselves to our strength and personhood. We can learn to let go of the sense of self that is attached to successful outcomes. It can be a very grounding reminder.

You see, being gutsy, being strong, has nothing to do with outcome. Sure, an outcome we perceive as *positive* is rewarding and feels nice, but it has little bearing on our inner strength. *That* has to do with showing up in the tough moments.

And what a powerful message this is for us mothers to model for our children. Let's think for a moment about how we want our children—our young daughters—to relate to themselves. We want our children to feel self-love and acceptance, not to base their own worth on feedback they receive from the world around them.

> "Sure, an outcome we perceive as *positive* is rewarding and feels nice, but it has little bearing on our inner strength. *That* has to do with showing up in the tough moments."

Now let's see if we can take a mirror to those desires we have for our children and reflect them right back onto ourselves. Sometimes it's easier to use the unconditional love we have for another as a conduit for the unconditional love we hope to have for ourselves. Can you take your children in as they are? If the answer is yes, you already have the blueprint for practicing this form of self-acceptance.

Fully embodying the beautiful message behind these words helps us learn to be okay with failure, with not meeting expectations, whether our own or someone else's.

Because if we truly learn to take ourselves in, take ourselves in *as is*, then context falls by the wayside. Because this phrase, *Will you take me in as I am?*, doesn't depend on if we did a good job, succeeded, or failed; it is learning to be present with ourselves and really, truly showing up for ourselves, just as we are, naked and unmasked. It is such a gentle, sweet turning inward of self-acceptance.

An important component to living our truth is *authenticity*. Allowing ourselves to be real with who we are. Ironically, when we are authentic, when we let go of fear of negative evaluation from ourselves or others, when we are less outcome driven, we benefit from increased self-esteem.[1]

Have you ever gone shopping and noticed a discounted item with an "as-is" tag? You love the style, but notice a small flaw (hence the discount). Despite the flaw, you take the item home and it grows to become one of your favorite wardrobe pieces. That's what this is like.

Several years ago, my mother gifted me my great-grandmother's engagement ring. It's a beautiful art deco diamond ring with one big-small flaw: it has a large chip in the center diamond. While this imperfection isn't noticeable if you don't know to look for it, it's one of those things that once you see, you can't unsee.

When I was first gifted this antique piece, while honored to have received it (I was named after this grandmother), a part of me felt sad about its defect. I wanted to make it better, shinier, "whole." I took it to a jeweler who specializes in antique jewelry to find out about replacing the stone. Something that wouldn't reveal imperfection every time the light caught it in a certain way. I often think about the advice that the lovely lady at the jewelry store gave me: "Honey [she said in the most genuine and endearing way], don't replace that stone—it's your great-grandmother's. She loved it. She wore it. Now you wear it." I took her advice.

Now, when I put on the ring, I reflect on this woman's wisdom. I see the flaw in the diamond and savor the added richness that it represents. It's history, it's love, it's being a link in a chain. It's more beautiful because of it. Sure, I have moments when the light catches the ring and I think about it not being whole. Then I remind myself that I am another woman in my family creating history and memories, displaying strength and bravery and the range of all human emotions, while wearing this ring.

This ring is one of my favorite jewelry pieces not despite its flaw but because of it. It represents nonattachment to outcomes as well as the depth and beauty of imperfection.

We are imperfect—we know that. It is the blessing of being human. Now if we could just love ourselves in our human condition, we would be in good shape. Perfectly imperfect.

> "We are imperfect—we know that. It is the blessing of being human. Now if we could just love ourselves in our human condition, we would be in good shape. Perfectly imperfect."

I think of the heroine in the movie *A Star Is Born*, particularly the moment when Ally steps into the limelight at her boyfriend's concert and rocks her song. We see it all played out on her face: the fear, the self-doubt, the decision to step onto the stage, and the triumph in facing that fear and following her dream. In the moment when she decides to step onto the stage, I imagine her whispering to herself:

Can I take myself in as I am?

Can I let myself be, in this moment, a version of myself that is connected to my goals, put down the limiting self-judgment, and accept whatever outcome this creates?

Barriers to Self-Acceptance

> "A good mistake is one we learn from and find value in."

Science shows that one barrier for self-acceptance is an inability to accept past mistakes.[2] But we're missing a wonderful opportunity for growth here: a good mistake is one we learn from and find value in.

Research has shown that carefully paying attention to our mistakes may actually help our future performance. In an interesting study, researchers found that analyzing past failure actually can increase future performance on a new task. These researchers found that when people were asked to write critically about past obstacles, they showed lower levels of cortisol (the "stress hormone") and made more careful decisions when confronting a new stressful task, which resulted in their improved performance. These findings suggest that it is beneficial to pay full attention to the setback, by writing or meditating about it, to help us find success in new endeavors. In short, having setbacks, and thinking critically about them (within reason and not in a ruminative kind of way), is actually *good* for us.[3]

It's important to undertake these reflections with a cushion of kindness, however. In another study, researchers found that people who thought they were responsible for breaking their own coffee cup gave up easier when asked to imagine how they would get coffee than those people who were told to imagine the cup was already broken.[4] Beating ourselves up for real or perceived mistakes acts as a barrier in pursuing our future. Harshly blaming ourselves is *not* the same as thoughtfully analyzing the situation and understanding where we went wrong. We also want to make sure our thinking is intentional and helpful. Circular, harsh, and judgment-based thinking is not what we are looking for here.

Let's make this idea a little more practical. Carve out some time to intentionally repeat back the phrase "Can I take myself in as I am?" Watch what thoughts pop into your mind as you say this to yourself. See if you can get in touch

> "Get in touch with the part of you that *knows* that you are okay. How can you take this self-acceptance with you into your life?"

with the part of you that *knows* that you are okay. How can you take this self-acceptance with you into your life?

Ask yourself again: "Can I take myself in as I am?" Notice what thoughts come up that may act as a barrier for self-acceptance. I find it helpful to connect to my body as I ask this question. Feel my feet on the floor or my back in my chair. Asking myself this question together with grounding myself in my body provide a powerful in-the-moment recentering.

I believe that self-acceptance has two primary roots: one that arises from an earlier and more primitive part that knows we are good—this part of us we are born with—and the other, from a later and experience-based part of ourselves that often has trouble believing in our inherent self-worth.

Lesson Learned from Improv

A few years ago, I started taking classes in improvisation.

I did this for a few different reasons. One, I had always dreamed of acting, but having been told that as a devout religious girl, this wasn't something I could pursue, I wasn't given the opportunities to try this as a child. Over the years, I buried that dream amid shame and rationalization.

A couple of years ago, on a women's retreat, I was talking about my long-held, deeply buried, *shameful* secret dream of acting and someone suggested I take improv classes. I toyed around with the idea for another ten months. I finally mentioned it to my therapist, who strongly encouraged me to do it. That very day, I signed up for my first improv class.

I loved it: it was fun, it was goofy, and I got to get up on a small makeshift stage, something I had yearned to do for as long as I could remember.

Fast-forward to the end of the second set of classes. We were each pulled aside to get some feedback on our improv skills. My instructor told me she thought I was "fun to watch" (imagine that!) and a "great supportive team player" (that makes sense). Her one constructive criticism for me was to "trust myself more." She noticed that there were moments where it seemed I would get stuck in my head and consequentially not fully participate.

My improv teacher, who had known me for a mere eight weeks, had picked up on such a core element of my personality. My tendencies to overthink and overanalyze were making not-so-cameo appearances in my improv work. Either I had a ridiculously intuitive improv teacher who moonlighted as a therapist, or this was something so deeply integrated into my core that it was apparent even to my acting teacher who barely knew me.

And this was exactly why taking improv has been so rewarding for me. It has pushed me into an area of greater self-acceptance—a more primal sense of *I am good*. It has forced me to acknowledge and limit the overthinking, unsure parts of myself that make an appearance every single time I jump onto the stage.

Now don't get me wrong. I still need to work on trusting myself every single improv session, but I do the work. I show up, get myself on stage, make myself jump out there to take a turn, and am learning to go with it and limit the headiness of how I play. Improv for me has become more than just something fun to do that started to scratch the acting itch; it's real-life, in-the-moment therapy for me in learning to trust myself and not overthink things. I recognize that my ability to listen, to really listen, without getting stuck in my head, is something I can continue to develop and use with all the people in my life—not just in an acting class.

At the root of being able to do that is some serious self-acceptance work. Accepting that I don't need to have the best and funniest response. Trusting that I have the capacity to come up with something on the spot. Knowing that I will be okay with whatever the outcome.

As a side note, practicing improv has ironically helped me work on my listening skills. I always prided myself in being a good listener. I'm pretty sure I've used that several times as a description of my strengths on both school and job interviews as well as on my past dating résumé.

I actually didn't realize until I started doing improv that while I *believed* I was a great listener, I spent quite a bit of time in my head planning my response while someone was talking. It's a profound experience to learn to put *that* process on hold and learn to *truly* listen: letting go of any thought or agenda (e.g., having something smart to respond with) and just be present and more spontaneous with the other person and their words.

Listening in that way opens the door for profound human connection within each conversation. Next time you have a conversation with someone, try this: Notice when you are getting stuck in your thoughts of what the other person is saying or—*gasp!*—you find your mind wandering. See if you could refocus and make eye contact without those thoughts clouding your vision. What happens to the connection you have with the other person? Does it shift at all? You can do this with anyone—your spouse, your child, the cashier at Trader Joe's (God bless them). It doesn't have to be weird, creepy, or soulful. It is just an opportunity for genuine human connection.

You Are Already Enough

I also learned that in improv, it is important to believe that *you are already enough.* Imagine that! If I wasn't sure I was in the right place before I heard the teacher say that, now I knew for sure.

This was the intro to the third improv session I did, and I loved it. For a moment, I wasn't sure if I was in a meditation class or an improv class, but I knew I must be in the right location, whatever it was.

The teacher started off by telling us that in the work of improv, our goal wasn't to try to be funny or chase something that wasn't there already. Then she added that revelatory kicker:

> **"We are already enough."**

Because we are already enough.

We already have in us, each one of us—from the naturally funniest people to me, who tells myself that I am naturally *un*funny when put on the spot—everything we need.

Beginning the experience this way made me readjust my expectations of this new class and this new teacher. I liked her, and I loved that message.

Self-Limiting

Early on in the course, I told my instructor, "By the way, I'm not really funny. I'm doing this for professional development to become a better public speaker."

Yes, I want to improve on my public speaking skills, but where did my notion—my *need*—to declare it to my teacher come from? There is certainly a self-limiting element to making such statements: *Oh, by the way—if I make a fool of myself onstage, you know, I already told you, I'm just not that funny. Just lower your expectations. Because me? I'm a bore.*

A certain part of me wanted my teacher to have low expectations so that when I was unfunny onstage, well, no worries, I already told her about my funny issue. But saying this to her speaks of something deeper. It is the limiting belief in my head getting in the way. The one that tells me, *Oh, other people are so much funnier than me. It's just not my strong suit.*

The uncanny thing is a whole other, quieter part of me *knows that this is not true.*

Even as I say, "Oh, tee-hee, I am not that funny," another part of me is arguing: "Yes, you are! Maybe not in the traditional, quick-witted sort of way, but you have a great dry and sarcastic sense of humor, not to mention a knack for noticing ironic and humorous things that happen to you (or your kids—sorry, guys) and the ability to vocalize it."

But here's the problem: the insecure thoughts are the ones that I paid much more attention to and bought so that they made the louder argument and were ultimately what I most easily believed about myself and told others.

And then what happens? A self-fulfilling prophecy. I feel insecure onstage in improv or large social gatherings and hold myself back from participating, or my improv teacher notices and tells me to *trust myself.*

As a side note, that is one of the powers of having support from other people: they point out your BS to you and make you face the stuff you might otherwise bury.

If I took more risk on the stage, chances are I would develop more ease getting out of my comfort level, share more without getting too stuck in my head, and get more laughs (not that that really matters, right?) because I am sharing more spontaneously, more freely. Then, most importantly, I would notice this and affirm to myself that I am having fun and this feels good. That I can do this.

That cycle there? That would be a *positive* self-fulfilling prophecy.

> "What we tell ourselves affects how many risks we are allowing ourselves to take. So a positive self-fulfilling prophecy opens up more and more possibilities."

This is what people are talking about when they talk about "mindset." What we tell ourselves can have more power over our outcomes than our actual abilities. Most people who are successful didn't just get there by chance. *Mindset* has so much to do with it. What we tell ourselves affects how many risks we are allowing ourselves to take. So a positive self-fulfilling prophecy opens up more and more possibilities.

What are you telling yourself that is holding you back from self-acceptance? How are you self-limiting?

Judgment and Social Comparisons

How often do you find yourself measuring your own perceived lack of accomplishments against someone else's success, home, children, relationship? This is what's known as social comparison.

Notice the tendency to do that, and try to shift out of it.

People who tend to compare themselves with others less report decreased guilt, regret, and blame.[5] In other studies, people who compared themselves to others more had lower self-esteem and satisfaction in life.[6] This is particularly true if the accomplishment that people are comparing themselves to is unattainable, whereas when it *is* attainable, those comparisons may be inspiring.[7]

Final verdict? Comparisons may be motivating for growth and behavior change but are not helpful sources for self-acceptance.

> "Comparisons may be motivating for growth and behavior change but are not helpful sources for self-acceptance."

So many of us compare ourselves to other people, most often in a not-so-flattering light. It's important to notice our mind's impulse to judge ourselves, acknowledge it when it happens, and just let it be while we shift away from it.

It's amazing how much we judge ourselves. Just pay attention to what your mind devises when you walk into a social event. Probably plenty of us start off the occasion with a proprietary evaluation of how we measure up against the others there. *Am I wearing the right thing? She always looks so put together. Shoot, I should've spent more time on my makeup. They always look so happy together.* Sometimes we can move from feeling spectacularly self-confident to astonishingly insecure in a matter of moments.

The culprit? Social comparison and self-judgment.

So it may behoove you to slow down and pay attention to those thoughts when they arise and make a mindful choice to enter into a wise relationship with them. It's okay that they are there—we are not trying to prevent their appearance. What we are doing is changing our relationship with them.

Now, ask yourself these questions:

Can I take myself in as I am?
In this very moment, with all that I am?
With my strengths, my challenges, my weaknesses and fears?
  Can I allow them to just be and withhold judgment?
Can I allow my humanity to just exist?

3

Our Stories of Our Worthiness

Can I be here now, with *just* this?

Many people, somewhere along the way of childhood, receive messages that make them believe they are flawed in some way. When we are children—who we believe ourselves to be—our strengths, our weaknesses, our place in this world largely come from messages we receive from the central people in our life. This means that what we learned about who we are stems from our parents, friends, teachers, siblings, and other influential people in our youth. These important figures have a huge influence on how our self-worth takes shape.

My heart still breaks every time I think of a session I did with ten-year-old Bobby and his mother. His mother was frustrated with Bobby's noncompliance and anxiety, and she was overwhelmed by other family circumstances. In one session, Bobby's mother was expressing her frustration. Bobby began to cry. And cry. I pointed this out to his mother several times, and she seemed oblivious or too caught up in her own frustration to notice Bobby's.

Bobby sobbed, "I just want to be good." Unfortunately, his mother was unable to hear this at the time and didn't provide him with the reassurance that he was good at his core. It was a sad moment, one where I felt somewhat helpless as a therapist watching these destructive dynamics taking hold. Of course, in the session I provided that reassurance and asked his mother to as well. But it was hard to know that these dynamics were present and taking root in Bobby's sense of worth.

Another client I worked with was seventeen-year-old Amy. Her parents had gone through a tough divorce, and Amy had questions about her mother's unconditional love toward her. This was especially tested when Amy's mother brought home a rescue rabbit—even after Amy had asked her mother not to do this. This started a cycle of resentment directed at that poor rabbit—who really wasn't rescued after all.

Amy needed to know she was her mother's priority, and sadly she didn't receive this reassurance from her. Her mother was adamant about keeping the bunny, not realizing what this represented for Amy and her mother's unconditional love of her. These are the sorts of situations that when repeated over and over again, in big and subtle ways, lead to fractures in our sense of worth.

These are lighter stories, comparatively, from the therapy world. I am not going to get started on stories of abuse and neglect I have heard from abandoned children living in the child welfare system. It is heart-wrenching and devastating to think of all these precious young, vulnerable people developing their sense of self in a broken, broken system.

This—our upbringing—is where beliefs about our self-worth develop from, my friends.

There are several modalities of therapy devoted to isolating and recognizing old beliefs we carry around with us and learning to rewrite them.

If we are lucky enough, the messages we got from key figures in our early development were healthy enough. This means that we grow into adults with a feeling of being inherently good and capable.

However, many people—like Bobby and Amy—have had at least one person important to them when they were a child give them messages that did not serve them, that led to beliefs about themselves that were negative. This could have been one parent, or both, or a sibling, or teachers, or peers, or anyone else with influence in their early life.

When we are children, we don't question what people tell us about ourselves because we don't know any better. So we adopt what we are told about ourselves as truths and thereon adapt to our environment within this framework.

We do this to get by, to survive.

If we are told we are defective in some way, we believe this to be true, since we don't have the wisdom or perspective to challenge important figures in our lives when we are vulnerable children. If we believe we are unworthy from the time we are children and conduct ourselves in this world based on this erroneous belief, we often don't challenge the belief. We assume it is true and act accordingly.

And you know what happens when we make assumptions, right?

> "The messages we receive as young children penetrate in a deep way, all the way down to our very core, and feel like truths."

We don't rock the boat, so to speak. We act according to these long-held beliefs and create outcomes that affirm them. The messages we receive as young children penetrate in a deep way, all the way down to our very core, and feel like truths.

The only issue? These beliefs are *not* truths. In fact, they were never, ever true.

I will never forget the work I did as an intern with a woman in her late sixties.

Her whole life she had believed she was intellectually challenged because of her struggle with dyslexia. She went to school before there was adequate education in the school system about people who learned differently and, therefore, before there were adequate ways to evaluate and accommodate them. Children who couldn't read because they had dyslexia were labeled "dumb."

When I crossed paths with her when she was in her late sixties, she only *suspected* it was dyslexia—because she had never been tested for it. She suffered through years of schooling where, because she had tremendous difficulty reading, she believed she was "dumb."

I remember a session in which we challenged this belief, this notion, where this woman started to question the authenticity of this decades-old belief. She had never thought to stop and wonder if this was true; she believed it with all her heart. It was only after exploring the origins of this belief that this woman had a light-bulb moment and understood where this belief stemmed from: not from truth, but from a flawed education system. I will never forget her tears of release as she sat with the realization that for years and years she believed that she was "dumb," and it was never true.

Let me repeat that. It was never, ever true.

Can you imagine the pain of waking up in your sixth decade of life and realizing that you lived a life of pain based on something that was never true in the first place?

For this woman, it was both painful and liberating. She began a new chapter in her relationship with herself. I suggested to her at the time that she has a ceremony of sorts, where she would honor the pain that the old belief had caused her and then symbolically place it in the water and watch it float away.

Right now, I work with many teenagers. It is refreshing and uplifting working with young souls who are getting ready to enter the world as adults. Many of these teens also carry around a host of beliefs about themselves. I see so many girls holding on to the trauma of being bullied or having one or both parents overemphasize what they were not doing right; I see them struggle with beliefs of not being enough, of being defective somehow, of being unlovable or ugly or untrustworthy.

It never fails to move me to see the shift when a person understands that they have a *choice* in what they believe about themselves and that they certainly don't have to believe that they are what some mean bully told them when they were in the fourth grade.

> "It never fails to move me to see the shift when a person understands that they have a *choice* in what they believe about themselves."

This is the power of the beliefs we have about ourselves.

Let's pause for a second and think: What are your beliefs about yourself? What beliefs serve you? These may be beliefs such as "I am likeable" or "I am successful" or "I am good."

Now pause again: What beliefs are *not* serving you? These may be beliefs such as "I am not good enough" or "There is something wrong with me" or "I will never be happy." Where did these beliefs stem from? You may even want to close your eyes and see what old memories surface for you. How old were you when you first remember feeling this way? Who fed you these toxic and untrue messages? Whose voice do you hear when these beliefs pop up, today?

Sit with it. Sit with it. Just let it sink in. Let it take hold that these messages, these harsh and cruel beliefs you feed yourself, were never, ever true.

Wow.

Can you identify the little you inside that still reacts with such sadness when these beliefs come up? Maybe try putting your hand over where you feel her inside your body. For me, I feel her right over my heart. Let her know you are here for her and that you will pay attention to her pain and sorrow. She is not alone. Not anymore. She may not have had the support she needed back then, but she does now. Because every single time she needs it, she will get that love and coaching from you. *You* get to give that to her when she begins to question her worth or lovability. It's an honor and a privilege to remind her of her innate, untouchable perfection, of the magic she was born with. And even though it may have *felt* lost along the way, it never was and never will be.

You may identify a hurting child inside of you, the one who yells out in pain when something happens *today* that triggers a painful set of old beliefs. This may happen when you get some constructive criticism at work, and just like that, this very understandable and ordinary life experience unleashes an avalanche of self-doubt and feelings of worthlessness.

When you have a strong reaction to a moderate or minor catalyst, this is a sign that there is a little you hiding just beneath the surface. A little you that gets brought to the forefront with the tiniest of triggers and is crying in pain. Next time you have a strong emotional reaction to something relatively benign, it may be worthwhile to pause and ask yourself:

When do I remember feeling this way when I was a child?

It is this question that will bring us the realization: *Ahhh, now this pain, it all makes sense. But I don't have to be wedded to it any more. I could learn to notice it as it arises and simultaneously compassionately embrace it, thank it for the protective role it played in my life, and set it aside.*

My Self-Worth

About seven years ago, a mentor of mine suggested I may benefit from a meditation retreat. At the time, the one I had my sights on was very difficult to get into because of its popularity. I was told it would fill up within moments of registration opening. Knowing this, I had arranged for myself and three family members to call in the moment registration for the event went live. The lines were busy for over an hour. My family—bless their hearts—gave up soon after they realized the lines would likely stay busy for who knows how long.

But not me. You see, even though it was a forgone conclusion for me that I wasn't going to get into the retreat, I thought I would at the very least get put on a waiting list. It was well over an hour later when someone finally, finally picked up the phone—and to my utter surprise, I got into the retreat.

Apparently, the phone lines had crashed and it had taken them this long to restore them. And so only the people who persisted in calling got in. It was absolutely meant to be. Some higher force wanted me on that retreat. I later learned that this was to be the last of this retreat being held with these particular instructors (which was important to me) and I remember the tears I cried at how fortunate I felt to be there.

(This is also an important lesson on the power of persistence!)

So there I was, on my first retreat, jumping right into the deep end, without fully realizing it. The schedule of this meditation retreat was pretty intense. Meditating beginning at 6:00 a.m., done for the night at 9:00 p.m., with the schedule of each day looking quite similar: rotating through different forms of meditation and silence, with a strong encouragement to limit phone use.

The purpose is to diminish distractions so that we may bring our attention to what is unfolding within us. Needless to say, participating in this sort of training lends itself to mind-blowing insights. Let me share one such awareness I came to during that retreat.

Silence came midway through the seven-day retreat and was to be observed for thirty-six hours. (Silence, by the way, extends beyond not talking. It is also recommended to avoid eye contact or read anything. It is meant to be a holistic solitary experience.) During the silent hours, I had ample time to notice my impulses, reactions, and emotional responses to what had transpired in the days before the silence began. I found my mind repeatedly going back to a bad feeling I had after I had offered a comment in the group the day before. I remember thinking I had something important to share, something that I was proud of. I raised my hand with my heart thumping in my chest—it's hard for me to raise my hand and share with a group of 150 people, let alone take a risk and offer a novel thought to this great meditation teacher whom I revere.

I got called on. I offered my insight and received a less-than-enthusiastic response from my meditation teacher. Not that it was a *bad* response—it was something along the lines of "Oh" or "Thank you." And then he moved on.

I don't remember what my comment was, but I sure do remember my emotional response at being met with a blasé reaction to my epiphany. I remember the heaviness, sadness, and shame.

I thought to myself, *Did I just say something stupid? What did others think of my comment? Maybe I shouldn't have said anything.*

Maybe I should observe silence for the rest of the retreat.

This incident happened at the beginning of the retreat, a couple of days before the silent portion. I had already moved on and was no longer consciously thinking about that experience.

However, during silence, the memory of this incident—and of my shame—popped back into consciousness. Now I had more time and stillness to notice, and reflect on, my patterns of thinking and behavior. I saw a trend within myself—my question-asking trend: I had a pattern of going over to the group leaders after sessions had ended to ask clarifying questions.

That wasn't my insight. My insight was that I was asking questions *that I already knew the answer to*. I wasn't doing it deliberately, and on some level, I really thought I had a

"If I had been listening, *really* listening to myself, I would have seen that I had the answers within me."

legitimate question. However, it was more a reflex than an actual need to fill in missing information. I was asking these questions quite thoughtfully, while subconsciously, if I had been listening, *really* listening to myself, I would have seen that I had the answers within me.

I came to the realization that by asking these questions, I was making a point of being validated by these great teachers, because their responses—their taking my questions seriously, the implicit or explicit feedback that I had asked a good question—those all made me feel good, that I *was* good.

I am not talking about "good" as in feeling "happy" or "content." I mean it in its most raw, primitive usage.

I felt *good.*

Their responses to my questions and comments validated that in fact, as a human, I. Was. Good.

I needed these external reminders to affirm that I was smart, that I was likeable, that I had good questions. That I was a worthy human being. The moment of eye contact was important to me as well. It made me feel seen.

And that's why the lack of an enthusiastic response to my comment during the group session elicited these big, strong feelings of shame: I didn't receive the external feedback and validation that on some level I needed so much, and I didn't yet have myself to lean on in terms of knowing my inherent goodness. I didn't yet know fully on a conscious level that I was, because of the very virtue of my being human (and so much more than that), *good.*

There was a moment where I realized so much of my experience in this world had the faint murmur and humming of "Am I good? Am I good?" in the background. It was there so much of the time *without me even realizing it.* Kind of like the self-defeating version of the Little Engine That Could's rhythmic "I think I can"—"Am I good? Am I good?"

After this realization, I found myself reversing the sentence. It transformed from a question— "Am I good?"—to a statement.

"I am good."

I. Am. Good.

I remember exactly where I was when I grasped this truth. I was on a beautiful overlook, the sun was setting, I was in the middle of a walking meditation, and I had the thought: *In this moment (after all, that's all we have for certain), I am good.*

We must affirm to ourselves our inherent goodness. This knowingness may start from our thoughts (if we struggle with this) but leads us within, to an awareness far deeper than our moment-to-moment consciousness, and most definitely not from any external source.

Perfectionists tend to judge themselves based on external validation of self-worth and are therefore more susceptible to psychological stress when they perceive negative events happening. Perfectionists are also less likely to have unconditional self-acceptance, and depression is associated with low unconditional self-acceptance.[1]

Knowing and embracing your innate good-ness is no joke, friends.

What does this mean? Accepting and acknowledging your worth *unconditionally?* Yep.

Most of us struggle with some sense of inner criticism— blame, shame, you name it—in who we are. Where this comes from is a book in and of itself, but in a nutshell, here goes my best summary:

We are born perfect. Imagine a little newborn baby. They are pretty perfect, right? They are tiny beings of immeasurable wholeness and miracles. They are magic. *You* were magic.

And you still are.

If we seek our sense of goodness from anyone other than ourselves, and to some extent even from the *thinking* part of ourselves, life becomes a big game of hopping from one validation source to another, like the Energizer Bunny. We are on a mission to prove something, but we never really get there; we only keep moving around in circles.

Where did my sense of not being good enough originate? The answer to that question is probably the contents of another book in and of itself, but I will get into it briefly. Because our stories *matter*—they become the fabric of who we believe ourselves to be and set us up on our life's journey.

> "When we give voice to our stories—the things that happened to us when we were younger—we begin to heal."

I hope that chronicling some of my narrative with you will create an openness for you to share your story with others. When we give voice to our stories—the things that happened to us when we were younger—we begin to heal. Furthermore, when we hear from others, we also recognize how universal our stories are, even while belonging uniquely to us. We begin to make more sense of who we are today and where our strengths and vulnerabilities may have developed from, and we realize that we don't have to tie ourselves to someone else's idea of who we are, which, quite possibly, was distorted and off anyway, having come from their own unprocessed injury.

So with that as a backdrop, I'll share some of my own story:

I am the youngest of five children. I was born in Denver, Colorado, and moved to Monsey, New York, when I was seven years old. I grew up in New York. My parents raised us under the Orthodox Jewish umbrella, they themselves coming to a more rigorous set of standards and taking on an Orthodox lifestyle after they met each other in college. Their religious observance was a big reason they moved the family back to New York, where they are both originally from. They wanted a larger Jewish community to raise us kids in. It was important to them that we were in more religious Jewish schools and part of a larger strictly Orthodox community.

Monsey is the home to one of the largest Orthodox Jewish communities in America—and probably the world, outside of Israel. I grew up in an Orthodox Jewish bubble: boys and girls didn't talk after they entered grade school, married and previously married women wore wigs to cover their hair, girls didn't wear pants, everyone ate strictly kosher food, we didn't listen to secular pop music or watch TV shows (although my family was more lax than some, and my siblings and I were allowed to watch G- and PG-rated movies at home; I missed out on eighties, nineties, and early 2000s pop culture—I joke with my friends that I "came of age" late to explain the big holes I have in my secular pop culture knowledge), and all our friends were very similar to us with little religious variation. We went to Orthodox schools and camps. Most every detail of our life was guided by religion. We said formal prayers two to three times a day in addition to blessings before and after we ate as well as after we used the bathroom or anytime we wore a special new item of clothing. The years were marked with several holidays where we couldn't use electricity for two or three days and had to leave lights on or off, or prepare all cooked foods in advance, or leave on the ovens for the duration of the holiday so as to be able to cook.

There were communal expectations for married couples to have a large family with many children. Girls, especially, were encouraged to marry young. I started dating for marriage at nineteen. By the time I married at twenty-three, most of my friends were married, and I felt like an old maid, desperately worried if I would ever marry.

I was born into this strictly arranged world, and I *thrived*. I was so religious. I didn't talk to boys—I didn't even *look* at boys (if someone was watching). I found mentors—rabbis and female teachers and my older siblings—to ask my life questions to so that they would guide me. I prayed long, emotional prayers. I followed all the strict rules of dress, covering up my body, from my collarbones to my knees. I wore tights in public so that not a spec of my leg was showing—not even my toes—and skirts to my all-female gym. Sometimes, I wore tights over my tights to make them even opaquer. I was valedictorian of both eighth and twelfth grades. I got a full scholarship to my (all-women Orthodox Jewish) college. I developed a reputation as a very smart, very religious girl.

Being very religious, my family lived an existence that revolved around "rights" and "wrongs," "shoulds" and "alloweds." But there was also internal family chaos, financial stress, and fighting.

Growing up like this, both without external stability *and* with a methodical equation of how to achieve "goodness," I adopted a system of verifying if I *was* good: so long as I clung to other people's expectations of me and found approval in their eyes, I was good.

I don't remember receiving many messages that I was *inherently* good, no matter whether I chose to conform or not. I felt that to be good, I had to live my life in a highly structured way that was subjected to the community's approval.

We all have different experiences with religion. It has been my experience that religion can offer us safety and reassurance when we follow a laid-out path. We are bestowed community, approval, a sense of belonging, and the promise that good will befall us, in this world or the next, if we follow the prescription. There can be a lot of beauty in being part of a religious community, as mentioned in the introduction. I fully appreciate how this brings meaning and security for so many, and believe many people are drawn to religion for this very reason. I have witnessed people who grew up with chaos come to religious practice and be comforted by the stability, assurance, and value it offers. After all, I think it is our human nature to crave certainty, and we are all drawn (at times) to the good feeling we get from being told what to do (certainty!) and the nice fuzzy feeling many of us get when other people are happy with us (ahhh, approval from others).

On the other hand, many of us do need to forgo some of our personal choice to stay happy and fulfilled within religious confines. Doing this can lead to what is called cognitive dissonance—having beliefs that do not match up with our behaviors. Being in a dissonant state can feel uncomfortable and confusing, as was my experience.

While acknowledging that the need for self-determination is dependent on the person (i.e., people may need this to different degrees), I firmly believe there is a place for both religion and owning our own life's choices. We can find this in balancing the value of choosing an individual path that brings personal joy and meaning while not denying the beauty of our own heritage and history.

Being Jewish is in my blood, my DNA. It's something I feel proud of, and I want to carry on this connectivity to my people and honor the struggles of my ancestors. And at the same time, I don't want to forgo the rich, fulfilling details of my life to make others happy with me. After all, we have one beautiful and short life to live. Let's make it as authentic, meaningful, and gutsy as we can.

These days when I reflect on my very religious upbringing, I believe there is true beauty in many of the customs with which I was raised, and I honor and cherish many of those customs. I also deeply respect individual thought and choice and being afforded the opportunity to choose our own path.

For me, the rigid nature of the religion I was brought up in combined with the de-emphasis of the self and my difficult childhood homelife resulted in my dealing for years with questioning and establishing my inherent value. I came into adulthood having learned to find self-worth and value from other people. If I was making them happy, I was good. I am now on an independent journey of self-discovery and self-worth and healing from loss at not having been offered this option in my more formative years.

Reclaiming my inherent worth, and helping others do the same, is a big part of my why (described in chapter 1). Personally, discovering the beauty and power in finding and redefining spirituality, and connecting and reconnecting with myself, has created a purpose and passion within me to help others do the same.

> "Oh, if you only knew (and I hope you do!) how beautiful, precious, gutsy, and worthy you have always been."

I think, to some extent, so many of us struggle with feelings of unworthiness. Whether or not religion is at its roots (i.e., the *context*), the *process* is the same: sorting through and understanding where these feelings developed and reclaiming our untouchable inherent value. Oh, if you only knew (and I hope you do!) how beautiful, precious, gutsy, and worthy you have always been.

What Is *Your* Story of Worthiness?

To access your self-worth, start by asking yourself these questions. It may be helpful to find a quiet space where you will not be interrupted to write down your answers.

What beliefs are humming in your mind? Do they serve you?

The ones that don't—begin to question them. Are they even true? (I'll give you a hint: no, they are not!) Where did they originate from? Can you go back to an early memory of where this belief originated? Can you identify a little version of yourself that still lives inside of you and cries when those beliefs come up? Whose voice are they, even? Most likely you will notice they are not yours but an early caregiver's.

Could it be that your strong reactions to current situations really have very little to do with what is happening right now and much more to do with what happened so very long ago? (Another hint: Yes. Yes, it likely does.)

We can start to acknowledge where our unhelpful thoughts and beliefs came from and not be beholden to them anymore. We can gently let them go as we create current, healthier beliefs. Slowly, patiently, lovingly.

This doesn't mean we should settle with where we are right now in life. This is not the message of "I. Am. Good." The message is that who you are—regardless of where you came from and what you accomplish in life—is amazing and magical. If you can use that belief as your starting place,

"This is the basic difference between self-esteem and self-worth. We develop self-esteem from our accomplishments; what we *do*. We never *develop* self-worth. It's something we are all born with, though many have to rediscover it."

anything is possible. This is the basic difference between self-esteem and self-worth. We develop self-esteem from our accomplishments; what we *do*. We never *develop* self-worth. It's something we are all born with, though many have to rediscover it.

If we are having trouble believing in our basic self-worth, it will be nearly impossible to accomplish our hopes and dreams. And even if you do outwardly accomplish your big goals, without the foundation of your self-worth, you'll still feel unfulfilled. We can't truly enjoy our accomplishments and success if underneath it all, they are only meant to prove something about our worth to other people. We do these things because, deep inside, it matters to *us*. It fills us up in a way only we can know and define. It is where we find our individual purpose and value.

It is important to keep in mind at all times that no matter what, who you are in this given moment is enough. You are already enough. You may be trying to accomplish a lot of big stuff in your life, and that is awesome. But remember—all those things have nothing to do with who you are at your core. You are already enough. You are already good. We stay connected to our passion and purpose and goals because they infuse our lives with *meaning*, not because they enhance our *worth*. See the difference?

Research indicates that we spend a lot more time than we might think giving our younger selves advice. Many people do this upward of more than once a week. They go back to a younger time in their lives and counsel their younger self. This process can be helpful to living a more fulfilling and actualized life.[2]

Getting in touch with our old stories, our old messages, can provide healing in different forms.

Ask yourself: If you could give your younger self advice, what would it be? How does doing this set you on a path *right now* that is empowered and fulfilling? And how about this: if younger you could counsel you today, what would they say? How might they encourage you to celebrate all that you've done so far that you never thought possible? In this life's journey, finding the balance between keeping our eyes on our next steps, dreams, and goals while maintaining a keen awareness of how far we have already come is where we meet ourselves with true self-love and compassion—and tender celebration.

> "Finding the balance between keeping our eyes on our next steps, dreams, and goals while maintaining a keen awareness of how far we have already come is where we meet ourselves with true self-love and compassion—and tender celebration."

Try saying out loud to yourself: "I am good, just as I am, right now."

Notice what comes up for you, and put out the welcome mat for whatever sadness or self-doubt might present itself. Now try saying the following:

Can I be here right now with just this?
With the most primitive part of me that knows my inherent worth and the other, newer parts of me that question that?

I will learn to acknowledge the thoughts and beliefs that are unhelpful and full of old pain as well as recognize how old they are.

I will practice noticing them as they arise, gently thanking them for at one time serving me, have compassion for myself that that was needed at the time, and then let them go, like the clouds in the sky.

And I will remind myself that I am good, just as I am, right now.

4

From Striver to Compassionate Being

You don't have to be good.

—Mary Oliver, "Wild Geese"

The first time I heard "Wild Geese" by Mary Oliver was on my very first meditation retreat—the meditation retreat I mentioned in the previous chapter. I distinctly remember closing my eyes and listening with openness and curiosity as the retreat leader read the poem out loud. I had liked all the other poetry so far: it was new and old to me at the same time; the words were new, while the concepts resonated deeply with truths buried in my soul.

But this poem hit me hard. I remember the floodgates of tears streaming down my face as the words woke up something deep inside of me.

You don't have to be good.

There it was: permission to step into myself and do what felt right and true to me.

It may seem funny to follow the previous chapter about knowing you are good with a line from a poem about how, actually, you don't have to be good. But the message of this poem to me is that we don't have to feel like we need to be good for anyone else or measure ourselves against anyone else's standards. We can let go the expectation to be the "good girl" or the "good boy." All my life I heard variations of "you have to be good." There wasn't much of a choice in my early world; the path to "goodness" felt linear.

Our community taught that following the laid-out path would lead to deep personal happiness and fulfillment, without addressing the possibility that this wouldn't be the case for everyone (though, surely it is, for many). In hindsight, for me it felt like being offered only the color blue, and having to choose between shades of blue for my whole life. One could surely find richness and depth in what was offered, and maybe even cautiously expand to digest a few extra shades if one needed more, but swathing oneself in the range of all colors was prohibited.

When we (or those around us) emphasize our image over the depth and acceptance of who we truly are (regardless of any outward trappings), we can become strivers. Needing to *be* a certain way to satisfy others and to be a constantly improving version of that is built into the values of so many cultures, religious and not religious alike. When we focus on the externals of who we are, we are missing really getting to know and appreciate who lives underneath the external. And that is really where we find ourselves. In a place way deeper than the exterior representation of who we are. With a curiosity born out of a gentle and compassionate excitement. Who am I? Who am I really? Who am I in this one moment in time? And the excitement and openness of what I will find tomorrow? The idea of being content with who we are deep inside, and loving ourselves as we are, as we will become, is a foreign concept for so many. We cling to the idea of who we should be or need to be for others instead of sinking into who we already are and allowing *our* inner evolving wisdom to guide that process.

One young adult I worked with, Melissa, came from an affluent nonreligious home. Her parents were both successful business people, and from the outside, their family looked picture (or Instagram) perfect. And in many ways, they were a healthy and functional unit. However, one of the main treatment goals in our therapy was helping Melissa work through the overemphasis on her image that she was raised with.

Her parents heavily stressed the importance of what the family projected onto the world, more so than encouraging each other's individuality and honoring their personal self-awareness. Melissa had so many old stories of the criticism she received about what she wore, who her friends were, and what she decided to pursue in college. This deeply affected her sense of self and confidence, to the point where she constantly questioned and felt doubtful in nearly all her adult choices. Our work together involved uncovering the origins of her self-doubt and included healing conversations with her family.

When we are raised to value appearance over happiness (in the deepest sense of this word), we are led far away from a deep knowing and honoring of ourselves. We learn to shelve brave and gutsy choices for the safer option of fitting in and being and doing what others want us to be and do. We get trained out of heeding this intuition and awareness and learn

> "When we are raised to value appearance over happiness (in the deepest sense of this word), we are led far away from a deep knowing and honoring of ourselves. We learn to shelve brave and gutsy choices for the safer option of fitting in and being and doing what others want us to be and do."

to find happiness from others, as opposed to following our own personal North Stars. This can set us up for years of frustration, sadness, and resentment, as it did for Melissa.

Striving

On the first night of a meditation retreat I attended, we went around the room sharing why we were at the retreat. Why we were really, truly at that specific retreat.

I took the microphone hoping the crowd wouldn't hear the thumping in my chest (remember, I get afraid to share things publicly—especially my more vulnerable, private thoughts). I said to the group, and my teacher, "I am here because the last time I was here three years ago, I had a life-changing experience. I felt lighter and surer of myself and more decisive. I want to get that girl back. I want that experience again, with the same results."

The retreat leader, with a lightness on his face, gently chided me: "Ah, but that is the root of suffering. Clinging."

That was it, and then he moved on.

My world came down and opened up wide before me, all at the same time.

He went on to describe that one of the sources of pain (according to Buddhist philosophy) was clinging, striving, attachment to an outcome. And this is exactly what I was doing, wanting to re-create an experience I had already had because of its profound effect on me.

This hit me like a ton of bricks, especially because, at that time, my identity—and a big source of my pride—was that of being a striver. Always doing more, achieving more, impressing more, and hoping to accumulate more and more successes, defined by a particular outcome.

The thing is, we cannot control outcomes. We have little say in so many of the variables that create an experience. Change is an inevitability of life. We all know this. And when we *need* a specific outcome and it doesn't work out the way we wanted, if we haven't accepted the certainty of uncertainty, this can be very painful. This attachment to results and perceived success can also be a big source of suffering.

Striving is the constant need to do more, be more, than what the actual moment is offering. It is doing whatever we need to do to secure the result we want and think we need. If overplayed, it leads to chronic discontent, self-judgment, and a harshness in how we live. When we are consumed with striving, we often miss what is before our very eyes and reinforce mistrust in ourselves and in our ability to handle challenging situations.

I have so many stories about the role of striving in my life. Some of them are funny retrospectively, but many of them are not. In the past, when I've gone on a retreat, I have always been one of the first to enter the meditation conference room in the morning to secure the perfect spot that would be mine for the whole day (no small feat considering the sessions typically start at 6:00 a.m., which feels like 3:00 a.m. to me, as I am usually jetlagged from flying to the conference). I would rush to the conference room intent on getting "my" spot and would feel pretty upset if someone else had claimed it. This was striving—I needed to curate the perfect experience because I didn't want to deal with the disappointment of things not going my way. But let me tell you, I would have benefited far more from letting go of the attachment to needing a particular outcome—in this case, the "perfect seat"—than what that outcome would have afforded me.

These kinds of stories make me chuckle because of the universality of them. I think many of us have had silly human experiences like that, where we got overly invested in some outcome that really seems unimportant after the fact. Although I laugh at such stories now, when we structure our lives around this way of living, we often feel anxious, disappointed, and stressed (and resentful toward others for getting in our way!).

> **"Knowing in this one moment, I am *enough just as I am,* and I am an evolving human being."**

It feels important to emphasize that "not striving" is *not* the same thing as complacency. I am not advocating we become self-satisfied, throwing up our hands and accepting mediocrity in ourselves or our relationships with others. We all have areas of improvement and change we'd like to see. And connecting to making change and working on ourselves leads to the richness of self-growth and development that is not only fulfilling but also exhilarating. I am not saying to give that up. What I'm advocating for is the tone we use and how we hold ourselves in both making change and celebrating who we already are. In being able to hold the duality of knowing in this one moment, I am *enough just as I am,* and I am an evolving human being.

And, the irony is, when we learn to embrace who we are in any given moment with deep love, compassion, and respect, making change is that much more possible. Because we are no longer encumbered by the unhealthy and faulty limiting thoughts that hold us back from showing up as our most authentic, brave, and gutsy selves. And when we learn to practice and embody self-compassion, we greatly expand on the compassion we are able to offer others.

We want to approach the rougher parts of ourselves with the "lightest of touches"—a gentle acknowledgment that those parts exist and what we can do to work on them balanced with allowing ourselves to "be." I recognize the irony here: the only way to allow ourselves to grow organically and kindly is to let go of striving *and* complacency.

Perpetual striving leads to never being satisfied with where we are in life and creates a strong attachment to how we think we *need* things to be. If we are that invested in how life should play itself out, we are setting ourselves up big time for much unhappiness and suffering.

Striving leads us to overthink and overanalyze the negative outcomes in life. And science shows that when we accept our negative mood states, rather than trying to be upbeat or change them in some way, we actually feel better. One study found that people who avoid the more uncomfortable emotions, like sadness, disappointment, and resentment, and even judge these feelings, feel more stressed. Those who allowed the feelings to run their course felt better in the long run.[1] Striving, attaching ourselves to some desired outcome, rather than accepting what is unfolding ends up making us feel worse.

Redefining Kindness

I didn't realize how much striving impacted my life until I was in my twenties. I was working with a therapist, an Orthodox Jewish woman, the woman who introduced me to

> "I was happy, but what I didn't realize at the time was that I was happy because it felt good making other people happy with me."

meditation retreats. I remember her using phrases like "You could get out of your own way" or encouraging me to be kind to myself. I genuinely didn't know what she was referring to. I had this concept of who I was and how I felt—and it was pretty great, based on the barometers that I used to measure happiness at the time. I thought I *was* kind to myself. I did what I was supposed to do, what others expected of me, what I thought God wanted of me. I was happy, but what I didn't realize at the time was that I was happy because it felt good making other people happy with me.

And this isn't real happiness. Happiness is something that originates and flows outward from within, not the other way around. It took me years to embrace the deep sadness that had lived inside me since I was a young child. I was deeply defended against my own sadness and loss, because I really, truly believed myself to be happy. Acknowledging my own sadness felt like a threat. Something that would make me a less "successful" individual somehow. And how sad (said in the most loving and nonjudging way) is it that I couldn't—wouldn't—honor my own deep and very real sadness. There is little quite as powerful and compassionate as honoring and accepting our feelings.

I struggled with the idea of redefining kindness as something that resulted from the delicate and compassionate way in which we treat ourselves, allowing ourselves to just *be* without judgment. It felt scary and uncertain to hold the reins of independent thought and decision-making and allow myself to investigate and pay attention to the sources of my unhappiness. Relaxing certain religious practices and choosing to live a life not completely sanctioned by my very orthodox culture felt like treachery, a worrying and impossible alternative. What is this notion of kindness? It felt like some kind of blasphemy.

Each of us will experience soul-turning moments in our lives, times when something happens and we feel an ethereal knowingness, as if the light of God is shining down on us. Often our lives become defined as "before this moment" and "after this moment." I experienced something like this that pivoted the direction of my entire life.

About twelve years ago, I had a phone therapy session with my Orthodox Jewish therapist. At the time, I had been married a couple of years and therefore wore a wig, as did my therapist, according to Orthodox custom.

I disliked wearing the wig. I disliked how subjugated it made me feel, I disliked that it was giving me a receding hairline at the age of twenty-five, and I disliked how I couldn't put my hair up in a ponytail and feel free and light. The wig made me feel heavy. I had felt this way about it from the very first time I had to don it. Sure, it made my hair look sleek and sexy, and now I was identified as a married woman by my community, which was an achievement I felt pride for.

But that's where my joy in wig wearing started and ended. I remember staring at myself in the mirror and thinking, *When I don't cover my hair anymore . . .* and catching myself, realizing with a certain amount of hopelessness and despair that I would always cover my hair. There didn't seem to be any other option. Dreaming about not doing it anymore was painful, because it felt like an impossibility. I had always been complimented that I had nice hair, and having to cover it felt so sad to me. (As a side note, some of my old friends will say they truly enjoy wearing their wigs. Again, we all have our own unique experiences.)

There is something profound here about the power of mindset. If we believe in ourselves, believe our dreams, then we are one gigantic step closer to realizing them. On some level, the sentence and thought of *When I don't cover my hair anymore* is part of what helped me actualize that dream. If I hadn't allowed myself to think of a "when," then I don't think I would be where I am right now, living a life that feels lighter, fuller, and happier, and on my own terms.

So back to my life-changing moment.

I was in the car, in the parking lot of my work, talking on the phone with my therapist about my struggles with covering my hair when she told me—and she rarely, if ever, told me anything about herself—that while she wore a wig to sessions, on her own time she didn't fully cover her hair. She wore hats but had the rest of her hair exposed for all the world to see.

I played it cool. I don't remember the rest of that phone session. But after we hung up, I sat in my car and cried. Big, long cries. Not sad cries, but cries of relief. Of permission. It was one of the first moments in my life when I *felt* life didn't have to be so hard and heavy. There was room for flexibility, for being different, for living a life that felt truer and more real and lighter for me.

In that moment, even though it was months before I started making my own changes, I started to understand what she meant by kindness. It meant flexibility, meeting myself in my areas of pain and making brave alternative choices not necessarily sanctioned by those around me. It meant giving up that nice and safe feeling I got from knowing I was doing the culturally appropriate thing for the exhilaration and lightness and deep satisfaction from knowing I was doing *my* thing.

I deeply respected my therapist—and, thankfully, so did my parents. She was referred to me by a respected teacher from my women's seminary in Israel. This therapist, who was my role model, told me about how she observed this commandment differently from the way I had been exposed to it.

Her sharing was the key that gave me permission to listen to myself and to step outside the expectations set forth for me by my family and community.

That's where my journey of religious self-exploration really began.

I allowed myself to pay attention to my questioning and start to *bravely* do things differently from how everyone expected me to do them. I began to uncover my hair— starting off by using my therapist's blueprint and wearing hats and berets. I bought myself a nice blow dryer as a celebration of this milestone. I can't remember many things as sweet as those first tastes of blow-drying my long, brown hair and proudly wearing it out or putting it up in a high pony with a baseball cap and going to the gym. I felt similar sweet tastes as I allowed myself to wear short sleeves and then pants. Then shorts. Those initial few times the wind brushed my exposed skin in public after I had spent years covering up was the most delicious feeling. I can still remember exactly where I was when I felt the sun kiss and the wind caress my arm (the parking lot of the Jewish Community Center in Portland) and that feeling of deep joy. To this day, noticing the breeze on my upper arm or the wind in my hair still makes me feel deeply grateful and connected— perhaps, strangely, to God and the universe.

Ironically, giving myself liberties allowed me to connect much more deeply with my religious practices. I knew that what I was doing was coming from my own choices and independent thought and from a place of my own truth and decisiveness.

As a young person, I felt like I needed to do things to make other people happy. This reinforced my self-doubt that, ultimately, I didn't know what was best for me. Nor did I feel that I had a safe option of exploring all possible scenarios that may have been right for me.

And therein lies the rub. Research indicates that people fare worse when they place more importance on extrinsic motivation ("I am doing this to make other people happy, for some external reward") versus intrinsic motivation ("I am doing this because it fulfills an innate psychological need"). People show decreased well-being when the focus is on external motivation.[2]

Getting in touch with and allowing your intrinsic motivation to lead the way is a true act of self-kindness.

Striving and Kindness

At a recent meditation retreat, when we talked about striving in meditation, we were guided to drop in the words *striving* or *nonstriving* when we noticed a punitive or judgmental inner voice as we meditated.

I loved this suggestion, because it helped me make sense of a deep frustration and discomfort I noticed as I would meditate. I would often notice a tightness in my chest and had a hard time being present in my body as I meditated. This would happen especially when I was attending to my breath, where I would feel so tense I would often unconsciously hold my breath as my mind wandered. Those physical experiences tended to coincide with my striving voice, constantly critiquing how I was meditating. The striving voice was literally limiting my oxygen, my ability to be at ease and just breathe.

Now I had a way of noting that voice, warmly and respectfully embracing her as the old friend that she is, having compassion for myself that she still shows up and maybe even thanking her for the adaptive role she played in my childhood, but choosing to no longer place her as my guiding star. I could affirm to myself that she is no longer needed in my life to help me survive. She has served her purpose, and I've got it from here.

My journey with meditation has highlighted how much the striving voice played in my mind. And gosh, was she punitive.

If I said the wrong thing, there she was, telling me, chiding me for not doing better. If I was having a hard time meditating, there she was telling me I was not doing it right.

If I was in a social situation where I didn't feel comfortable, there she was telling me I was not enough; I was too meek.

This awareness brings along with it a sacred responsibility though. While the development of this striving voice may have her roots in my upbringing, what I choose to do with her now, in my adult life, rests fully and squarely on my shoulders. It is my obligation, my piece of showing up and living bravely, to pay attention to these harsh thoughts and not be complacent in my suffering; this is *my* revered duty now.

And there is true power in acknowledging that. In using compassion for our young selves as a nod to where things *started* and continuing that compassion by taking accountability for where things *are*. In this lens, taking personal responsibility for our lives, in their current state, is a true act of self-compassion. We can't do anything about what was, or how we were raised, but we sure as hell can take the steering wheel: Right. This. Very. Moment.

Perhaps taking compassionate accountability for ourselves— our thoughts and behaviors—holds the greatest key to personal power and the possibility of change because loving accountability opens the biggest doors to making change,

> "Loving accountability opens the biggest doors to making change, allowing ourselves to process the past *and* make brave commitments to our future."

allowing ourselves to process the past *and* make brave commitments to our future.

My striving voice is outcome attached. And attachment is the root of suffering. She wants things—*me*—to be a certain way. She wants me not to make mistakes, to come across a certain way, and to know what to say and when to say it. She wants me to experience things the way that *she* wants me to.

The problem with heeding the voice of the striver, and letting her guide our next moves and how we feel about ourselves, is that it often leads to a painful life. It leads to suffering. It's a heavy way to live because we are not perfect. We make mistakes. We say the wrong thing. And sometimes we hurt people.

I know *I* do.

But the striver—the voice that often starts with the words *you should* or *you shouldn't or why did you?*—is the voice we need to notice more and more so that we can pause, recenter, and get in touch with a deeper part of ourselves that *knows*. Because "should" and "shouldn't" are thinking traps.

Those are not friendly, helpful thoughts. It's either water under the bridge, or if it's something important to us, we better commit to it with an "I will" or an "I won't." The "shoulds" and "shouldn'ts" so often beat us up and make us feel bad.

The "I wills" reflect commitment to a choice and to ourselves. They signify an openness to taking healthy risks and managing the outcomes—good *or* bad. These choices come from an inner knowing or wisdom that not only are we capable of good judgment but we are also equipped with resilience should things not go the way we had hoped them to. You can try this out now: take something you need to do, such as calling a friend to check in on them, or something you are working on in your parenting, and see how the sentence feels when we replace the word *should* with *will*.

Changing *I really should call this friend* to *I will call this friend* feels different coming out, doesn't it? Or *I really should work on not raising my voice at home* to *I will work on not raising my voice at home*. One is a subtle judgment and reflects an indecisive noncommitment, but the other is more resolute, coming from a place of knowing and decisiveness that stems from your values.

It isn't important, the "should" or "shouldn't." What's important is what happened—the "is." This *is* what happened. This *is* how I feel about it. This *is* what I will do about that, and that *is* okay.

And now what?

It's incredible how many thoughts we have running through our heads all the time and, for so many of us, how harsh a lot of them can be. It's even more eye-opening when we choose to pay attention to them and realize just how frequent and just how cruel these thoughts can be.

For me, in the beginning of my mindfulness practice, I was surprised by the constant stream of punishing thoughts I was having that revolved around striving and self-judgment—and that I wasn't even aware of them much of the time.

This striver, the one who tells us we are not enough, can also be at the root of our lack of compassion toward ourselves.

In contrast, practicing mindfulness has been shown to increase self-acceptance, as one study illustrated: after participating in mindfulness training, participants had less of a gap between their actual self (who they believed themselves to be) and their ideal self (who they aspired to be).[3] This indicates that mindfulness helps people become more comfortable with who they presently are.[4]

During a silent portion for that first seven-day retreat, I remember washing my face in the morning while getting ready for our 6:00 a.m. meditation. I splashed water on my face, as I had done thousands of times before, and put on my face cleanser—the very same one I have been using since high school. As I was applying the cleanser, I was hit by how hard and abrupt I was being with myself as I washed my face, applying too much pressure for the task at hand. I hadn't ever realized that in my haste to get ready in the morning rush I was shockingly harsh with *my own face.* I stopped, shocked. I caressed my face gently, more compassionate as I completed the job of washing my face.

How many times do we go through the motions of daily self-care tasks—washing our faces, for example—without realizing how we are being with ourselves, how we are treating ourselves?

It's as if the implicit message we are sending to ourselves is "Hurry along, get it done, onto the next thing. You are not that important."

> **"Participating in the care of your body with mindfulness lends itself to a gratitude and warmth toward your body that is just lovely."**

Play with this concept in your life. Notice touch—the pressure you are investing in any given task, but especially the ones involving caring for your body.

Next time you are washing your face, or shaving your legs, or some effort in self-care, notice how you are as you take care of your body. Are you loving and compassionate and tender? Or abrasive, mindless, and rushed? Participating in the care of your body with mindfulness lends itself to a gratitude and warmth toward your body that is just lovely.

Relatedly, how many times have you looked in the mirror and *without even realizing it* had harsh and cruel thoughts about your reflection?

> *Ugh. I really need to lose some weight.*
> *Oh great. New wrinkles and white hairs.*
> *Look at that pimple on my face.*

I realized I had been catching glimpses of myself in the mirror, and sadly, my thoughts weren't *You are so lucky to have this amazing, miraculous body!*

No. Most of the time, the initial thoughts (and perhaps *only* thoughts) I was having *about my one precious body* were thoughts of harsh criticism and shame.

The striver, telling us we aren't enough.

"The striver, telling us we aren't enough."

The striver, making it difficult for us to appreciate our own power and strength that is already there—and has always *been* there.

I believe it is this voice, too, that makes it hard for a lot of us to practice basic self-care.

We all know someone (maybe it's ourselves) who is aware that they are neglecting their physical or mental health in some way, and yet they choose to stay in the self-destructive cycle. It is such a frustrating and painful dynamic to watch—especially if this is someone you love.

The pain of witnessing someone you care about behaving in uncaring and damaging ways toward their bodies is difficult. I see this often with my clients, especially the teenagers. They feel stuck and helpless watching a parent make poor health choices. Much of our work in therapy is helping them find their balance between expression, communication, and acceptance that they can't change their parent's choices. Or the reverse of that: parents watching as their young adult children make poor and destructive choices about their health and wellness.

One young woman I was treating, Sam, was a junior in high school. She struggled with anxiety and depression. Some of it was innate, but much of her anxiety and feelings of hopelessness surrounded her mother's choice to drink too much and smoke while dealing with untreated health issues. Sam loved her mother very much, so in our therapy, we processed Sam's pain and fear about her mother's choices, found ways she could make room for acceptance of what was out of her control, and reminded her of where her power lay.

Let's turn that same concern we have for others in our lives inward. Let's feel a tender pain (fueled by great, deep self-love) at our own disregard of our bodies and use that as a catalyst to make changes for ourselves. After all, we all know the clichéd phrase: the only person you can change is yourself.

I have seen so many campaigns on social media to remind us all to hydrate. There is a whole market of water bottles with reminders about how much to drink during the day. Do you struggle with hydration? I know that despite the fact that I carry around a water bottle with me everywhere (I'm not exaggerating), I often forget to drink from it. We neglect out bodies in this most fundamental way, and one has to wonder, why? What's beneath that basic lack of self-care and love?

Beyond water, how might you be ignoring your body's signals to take care of it?

Maybe you wake up sleepy and grumpy in the morning because you consistently go to bed too late due to bingeing Netflix or being up late working on a project. Maybe you continually make poor eating choices because you are ravenous from skipping meals earlier in the day. Maybe you constantly have aching feet and blisters because you persist in wearing shoes that are uncomfortable. Whatever it is, it is important to heed the body's communication.

Let's listen to our bodies. We get feedback all the time from them, letting us know how we are doing in treating them. If we slow down and learn to heed this information, we are building self-compassion and acceptance. These qualities will carry forward into other areas of our lives.

> **"Let's listen to our bodies. We get feedback all the time from them, letting us know how we are doing in treating them."**

A client shared with me that he had an epiphany: for lunch, he used to make himself a basic sandwich. At one point, he realized that *he deserved* a deli-grade sandwich with all the fixings. He described that in taking the time to prepare himself a beefy, thick sandwich, he felt loved. By himself.

I believe taking care of ourselves in this way has to do with kindness and self-compassion, and our relationship to the striver. When we are wired up and living in Striving Land, we don't focus on self-care or self-love. The striver is at odds with the practice of self-love, telling us that who we are at the root of it all is not enough.

Why would we value nurturing ourselves if we believe we are inherently unworthy? We can change this self-destructive cycle by rewriting these false beliefs *and* by taking action that affirms our worth. It's not easy, no. It's not immediate. But with time, patience, work, and love, it is possible.

Drinking water is an act of self-love, perhaps one of the most primitive we can show ourselves. How are you with drinking water? If it is difficult for you to keep yourself adequately hydrated, why do you think that is? How can you affirm your self-worth with how you choose to fuel your body? The way I see it, by keeping ourselves hydrated, we are pouring—*washing*—ourselves with love and compassion.

You know why you don't have to be good? Because you *already are good.*

You always have been good. You don't have to be anything other than what you are to be complete and whole and good. You don't need to be any different. You were born good. You are good.

Don't let anyone talk you out of that. Especially not yourself.

5

As I Am

I am here.

Meg, a woman I worked with in her twenties was struggling with ongoing obsessive thoughts that always had the theme of her believing she was a bad person. Even though the content of her obsessive thoughts varied a bit, the premise of her believing herself to be a terrible person was always there at their roots. In our work together, we used a lot of the effective cognitive behavioral therapy skills, including exposure and response prevention, known to be the gold standard in treating obsessive compulsive disorder.

These skills helped Meg learn to become her own expert at managing her obsessive thinking. Doing exposure work with obsessive thoughts can be an effective tool in learning to become unafraid of them, diffuse their power, and recognize that a thought is just a thought. Nothing more, nothing less. We don't have to buy into the illusion that they are big and mighty and threatening. However, aside from the work we did with her obsessive thoughts, Meg also held on to limiting beliefs about who she was as a person.

Her work was enhanced as she understood where her feelings of not being a good person may have stemmed from (messages she received from her parents and bad early educational experiences) and how she could let those defunct old beliefs go and redevelop a healthier and more accurate understanding of herself. This work was part of a secondary treatment goal: learning to build greater self-worth and an understanding of where some faulty conceptions she had about herself developed from. In this part of the therapy work, we discussed self-identity, core values, and beliefs, always holding these discussions on the foundation that we are ever changing, and Meg's knowledge of herself would evolve, change, and grow through different life experiences.

"We can't fully have compassion for ourselves if we don't know ourselves."

We can't fully have compassion for ourselves if we don't *know* ourselves. Oftentimes, the faulty belief that we are not inherently good comes along with anxiety and depression. As mentioned earlier, these notions are not only false but also stem from messages you were given by another human early on in your life. Part of working through these painful self-beliefs and learning to treat ourselves more compassionately is committing to a deep and evolving friendship with ourselves. And a significant component of deep connection is a deep knowing. One way to think about this is that one of the very best ways in which we show love to the people closest to us is by paying attention to them, expending the time and energy to really getting to know them. Offering the same gentle but focused curiosity to ourselves is an act of self-love and care.

Don't forget: who we know is the person in this moment in time, and we all change. Just as the seasons change the nature around us, the passing of time changes us too. It is an inevitable (and profound) life's truth.

Self-identity is one of those funny ironies. It is important to know who we are, to have our best relationship with ourselves, and part of this knowingness is an acknowledgment of the conundrum of knowing we can't really know who we are. We may have a cognitive frame for who we think we are, but underneath that lives awareness, like the vast sky: awareness of our thoughts of who we think we are, awareness of how certain things make us feel, awareness of what our values might be, and so on. But what really is awareness? Or the place from where awareness stems? It's a timeless conundrum. I don't know an answer, but for the following discussion, we'll focus more on the cognitive frame within which we know ourselves.

So: Who are you?

Who is it that dwells inside your body right now?

I don't think there is an easy answer for this. Identity, who we know ourselves to be, is a fluid concept. We think we know who we are, and then we come to surprise ourselves in the discovery that we may have changed or that we never were what we had assumed ourselves to be.

This perhaps is easier and more common to realize in our partners, for those of you in longer-term relationships. One day, we realize the person we are with is very different from the person we committed to years ago (especially those of us who married young). As a product of being human, we evolve, change, and mature. It takes more of an intentional sitting to tune into our own evolution, but I guarantee you, it's there, and it's often very, very beautiful.

For a long time, I believed I was one way. Come to find out, I was actually quite different and needed to have different experiences in life to understand that.

For example, I always assumed I was an extrovert. I'm not. I like people and enjoy engaging with others, but I deeply appreciate my alone time. As I have grown and matured, I also learned more about my grit and tenacity.

One of my most rewarding therapeutic experiences is when I have the privilege of working with individuals over several years. As we reflect from time to time on their growth and evolution, often marked by milestones (*Do you remember how you experienced this holiday last year? Look at how far you've come*), I inevitably grow teary-eyed. Watching our own and others' capacity to change and evolve is powerful. I remind my clients that, indeed, they are their own change. They are the force that showed up to make healthy and brave new choices that led to positive change and growth.

> "Be interested in your inner inclinations and desires and you will learn a whole lot about yourself."

Can you open yourself up to the possibility of finding newness within? This is where practicing openness and curiosity about yourself comes in. If there is something you have been wanting to explore or learn about, go for it! Be interested in your inner inclinations and desires and you will learn a whole lot about yourself. You may find you love whatever it is, just like you had always imagined, or much to your surprise, you may find you hate it. Practicing curiosity can be trying anything new—food, clothes, hobbies, or even just taking a new way home from work. If we are curious about ourselves and this life, we can truly get to know who we are in this given moment.

Let playfulness, and a sense of adventure, cushion your curiosity. There is something exhilarating in finding out fresh things about yourself.

Being curious has been linked to well-being, meaning, and satisfaction in life.[1] It has also been linked to physical health and more satisfying social interactions.[2]

Get in touch with your values—the things that give your life meaning and give you a boost in your step—and practice them! This becomes part of your identity. If you value helping your community, sign up to volunteer in your child's school or on a committee through your religious institution if you have one. You are taking a value—something abstract—and making it concrete, a behavior, and with practice it becomes a part of who you are and how you define yourself.

Not all pieces of identity can be expressed in a behavior. Your thoughts, your feelings, and the sum total of them translating into your perception of the world—*that* is a piece of your identity, too.

Ask yourself these questions. Write down your answers. It will likely be gratifying. What are your likes? Dislikes? Character strengths? Weaknesses? What are some things you believed about yourself that it might be time to reexamine? What are some of the missions you feel are yours to accomplish in this world?

And after that, try a practice of drinking more water. Do it with the intention of self-worth and self-love. Maybe recite this to yourself out loud before you drink: "I am drinking this water because I am worth it."

In my Jewish tradition, it is customary to recite a blessing before and after all food and drink. We thank God for the food we are about to eat or drink, recognizing he is the source of the food. And we thank him when we are done. It is a beautiful ritual. Let's generalize this and start a similar intention, where before we drink water, we say out loud (or in our heads) an affirmation that we are deserving of this water and drinking this water is an act of self-love.

"I am drinking this water because I am worth it."

You Are a Person outside of Your Relationships

This is important when it comes to self-identity. We are surrounded by people, many of whom we may be in close relationships with: our children, our significant others, our parents, our siblings, and our friends. Having relationships, being connected to other people is incredibly important (more on that later). That being said, though, as clichéd as this may sound, the number-one relationship in your life needs to be with yourself. We are happier, healthier, and, ironically, enjoy more fulfilling relationships with other people when we have an awesome one with ourselves.

It is so easy to lose sight of who we are outside of our most intimate relationships, especially those with our significant others and children. Because of the intimacy we share with these people, not to mention the time and energy we invest in these relationships (which can take up many of our resources), we can easily lose sight of the amazing, *independent* individual who lives in and around those relationships.

I know I have had years where I was so focused on my relationship with my husband—the highs *and* the lows— that I lost track of a lot of who *I* was, independent from my relationship. I had an epiphany a while back that *I am a person outside of my marriage* and that I need to pay attention to that person, just as I do this with the other most important people in my life.

For some of you, this may sound basic because you already live this reality. For others, it is a surprisingly easy concept to forget. For years, I had been so consumed with the identity created by my relationships (wife, mother) that I forgot that, ultimately, I am responsible for creating my own identity. Yes, I am a wife. I am a mother. And I am Leah—in those relationships and in the spaces between them.

That's why it is so important to have hobbies, values that are just yours, and time spent only on yourself. Maybe these are things that spoke to you before you got married or had kids, or they are new things that have only recently arrived on your radar. This was the impetus for me to start my improv classes, invest myself in my mindfulness practice and training, write this book, and develop new friendships. Doing these things are a reminder of my personhood and, quite frankly, are exhilarating, grounding, and fulfilling.

The one person you are guaranteed to have for your lifetime is you—best get to love and know that person. This is something no one can take away from you: the relationship you have with yourself and the attitude with which you choose to approach this life.

> "The one person you are guaranteed to have for your lifetime is you—best get to love and know that person."

I often hear people frame self-love and compassion as selfish somehow. This couldn't be farther from the truth. Self-compassion increases our ability to be compassionate toward others. Self-love and self-compassion start with you but certainly don't end with you. They are not the same things as self-indulgence. They will deepen your relationships with others, they will model for your children how to love themselves, and they increase efficiency and creativity. They will be the catalysts with which we can most fully and authentically change ourselves and—not to be too corny here, I really believe this—change the world.

Try saying out loud to yourself:

I was born good, am good now, and will always be good. I am good, and I don't have to be good for others.

There is an inherent goodness within me simply by virtue of me being. Nothing and no one can ever take that away from me.

I can take on life's challenges and know I am capable of so much and, at the same time, hold the awareness that who I am right now, in this very moment, is enough.

I will learn to love my body with all that it offers me.

Part 2

When the roots of a tree are strong, the tree is solid and can weather harsh storms. Focusing on *our* roots—the *kishkas* (inner workings) of who we are—sets the stage for us to start really, truly, stepping into our bravery, living a life of gutsy, authentic action and perspective.

The next part of this book is all about attending to the trunk and the leaves: the behaviors and outlooks that lead to building a beautiful and brave life for yourself.

Embracing Change

We can practice self-care. We can practice kindness and work on our self-worth and confidence. But even if we master these ideas, if they only live in our minds, then we are stopping short of what we are *truly* capable of.

Really *embodying* your own self-worth involves a *knowing*—and also a *doing*. We need to *do* the *actions* to make abstract values a living, breathing part of our realities.

So why do so many of us feel stuck at this crucial step—taking action—in one way or another?

Because change is scary and hard. We've discussed how attachment is at the root of suffering, making change painful and uncertain, even when this change leads us to a healthier path.

Change means stepping into the unfamiliar. This is never easy, even with the changes we crave the most.

Think of the big changes you have encountered on your journey in life so far: a new job, having a baby, getting married. These are all amazing things, changes that have been (hopefully) for the better.

However, think back to when they were actually happening. I suspect you probably felt a lot of fear and stress surrounding those big life changes. In fact, major life changes—like getting married or moving—are at the top of the list of life's biggest stressors, even if they are *positive* changes for all the *positive* reasons.

I think of all the high school seniors I have treated who are experiencing significant anxiety over going away to college. Or the anxiety many children feel before they start middle school or high school. Or the clients who feel stressed and worried about a new job, a move to a new house, or a child getting married. Or how so many of us feel on Sunday night, before we jump into a new work week. Transitions are inevitably difficult.

Why is change so stressful? Because change is scary and leads us into the unknown. It takes *bravery* and *gutsiness* to change and cross the line from the familiar to the new.

And that is what is really at the core of the messages in the next chapters: accessing the bravery that lives inside of you so that you can take actionable steps toward a new life. We all have the ability to be gutsy, to make change, but for some of us that ability may be so clouded over it feels like it's not there at all. When someone—a client, a friend—tells me that they are not brave, it hurts. Because we are *all* brave and have the capacity to embrace change. If you don't think you are, it's because somewhere along the way, your bravery has gotten covered up by muck—most often, other people's muck.

In my therapy work, I emphasize with all my clients their strength and their bravery. Just showing up for a session? That takes guts and bravery, especially when the content of the session may very well be hard or feel embarrassing.

Several teenage girls whom I work with are struggling with anxiety and depression and have been let down by adults in the past. Opening up to me, their therapist, risking being let down again by another adult? That takes bravery. It takes bravery to make change.

Some of the most emotional sessions I have had with the teenagers I see are when the teens open up about their identity, such as coming out as gay, bisexual, or transgender. Often, their immediate family doesn't know yet, and only a smattering of very close and safe friends are aware of what the teen is dealing with. Teens in the middle or end of high school have come out to me as gay or trans and have told me that they have known since they were in middle school that they didn't conform to traditional sexual orientation or gender roles. For these teens, coming out to me—to *any* adult or person—is bravery and is a powerful step in making positive change in their lives.

Similarly, starting to talk about old trauma takes an awful lot of bravery. Sometimes, this trauma has been buried for decades, and the individual was doing well enough. The choice to acknowledge and address old pain in the efforts to make life feel better and get vulnerable with a trusted individual is a tremendous act of bravery.

It fills me with deep emotion and acknowledgment of the privilege and responsibility I have in creating a safe space for people—younger and older alike—to be fully open with who they are and where they have been. My clients' bravery—their willingness to make gutsy, actionable change—takes my breath away.

6

Tossing Old Scripts Aside (in Favor of Newer, Healthier Ones)

I've done scary things before.

I'll never forget the first time I saw the movie *Frozen*.

Little did I know that would be the first of, like, a *gazillion* times I would see that movie—if you're a mother, you're probably in the same boat!

I sat down to watch it for the first time in the theater with my three-year-old son, thinking it was an ice age–era movie about a snowman and a reindeer. I was *not* prepared for how this movie would emotionally affect me. I remember sitting there in the dark cool of the theater and crying when Elsa sang the now-(in)famous song, "Let It Go." I cried because her story resonated with me. Well, not the part where she has uncontrollable ice powers and builds herself an amazing ice castle. But the part where she was taught to hide something that is inherent to who she is—in her case, by her very own parents. She carries the blame of her sister's near-death for years and feels that because of her ice powers, she is *defective* and *bad*. And she must hide it at all costs from anyone else on the planet. Her parents, though well-meaning, reinforced these ideas about who she is and unfortunately died before they were able to have any sort of discussion about it.

So Elsa grows up thinking that at her very core, she is defective. So much so that she must hide from the rest of the world lest they discover who she really is. When Coronation Day arrives, as much as she has practiced keeping those "ugly" truths about herself hidden, they come spilling out for all to see. She is exposed in front of a huge crowd of important people and can't handle the worry and fear of what everyone is thinking about her vulnerability.

Elsa's evolution in the song "Let It Go" is remarkable: we see a different Elsa emerge, one who comes to terms with how she was created. She even learns to *celebrate* her difference. We see her building her amazing castle and changing into a glamorous gown. Her hands are no longer covered up by gloves; she is free and finally able to be who she has always been.

All in the span of a three-minute song, she lets go of a defunct old script (I am bad; I cannot be myself in this world) and steps into a newer, more rewarding one (I have amazing and unique powers). She says, "Something has changed within me"—she is no longer willing to live a life where she is hiding in plain sight. This was the first step in Elsa's work (oh boy, I would have loved to be her therapist!). She still needs to learn to be her authentic self with other people. Her work of self-discovery and acceptance is finished at the end of the movie when she allows herself to come back to society and live among her people, in all her frozen glory.

So, I'm in the theater hearing this song for the first time, and I'm bawling like a baby. Her song hit me right in my heart. It resonated with my story—how I felt as though I was meant to *do* things and *be* things, even at a young age but was taught that those desires were not acceptable. I felt that I had to cover them up and be someone who made the people around me happy and comfortable, not who I felt I was meant to be.

And because of my nature—being a pleaser, wanting to make other people happy—I did precisely that. I was who other people wanted me to be, in very big ways. This became one of my most self-sabotaging scripts.

What we tell ourselves we are capable of is *very* important when it comes to making changes in our lives. If we want to bravely make changes, we can cultivate scripts to affirm our strength.

> "If we want to bravely make changes, we can cultivate scripts to affirm our strength."

Studies show that students do significantly better in school when they believe they are capable of more intellectual success.[1] People who tell themselves that they are unmusical (regardless of the veracity of the statement) deprive themselves from future engagement with music and future enjoyment from making music.[2] The lines our mind feeds us—and the ones we choose to heed—indeed affect us.

Developing a positive *script* is different from cultivating positive *thoughts*. Positive thoughts are more situation-specific, creating positive thinking to challenge faulty thinking as it arises. For example, a positive thought in response to getting some negative feedback at work might be "This was only one comment. It's natural to get negative feedback sometimes. Look at all the positive feedback I've gotten over the years." We are cultivating more resilient thinking in this one situation that is context specific.

A positive *script* is a go-to thought pattern that you learn to call on in difficult situations. It is similar to a script you'd rehearse and memorize for a play. The goal is for your script to become foundational, even automatic—something you call on over and over to help you get through sticky situations and overcome self-doubt.

Negative scripts are the opposite: lines we have rehearsed that reinforce we are not capable of being brave. Things like:

I can't do this.
They are judging me.
I cannot handle failure.
I'm not good enough. Other people know better.

It's amazing how often these same old scripts are there, playing in our head, *without us even realizing it.* And these self-defeating scripts guide us along on a less-than-fulfilling journey.

An important component of being brave is developing your own resilient script. Something along the lines of:

I can do hard things.
I'll get through this; I've gotten though tough stuff before.
This, too, shall pass.

All feelings, thoughts, and situations are transient.
I am strong.
I've done scary things before.
I am surrounded by people who love me.

It may be helpful to reflect back on the times in your life when you were brave and strong.

See if you can isolate the thoughts you had running through your mind that allowed you to be brave in those moments.

That time you set a boundary with a difficult family member? That was bravery. What did your mind produce that allowed you to you do *that*?

When you went back to school after having been out for quite some time? That was courage. What thoughts helped get your heinie back *there*?

Quitting the job that wasn't working for you and was toxic? That took *guts*.

Continuing a training position with a boss who was difficult and learning skillful ways to get through the experience? That was bravery, too (a true example from my life).

Having a baby? Well, *geez louise*, it doesn't get much gutsier than that!

What are some things you have done that were gutsy? Today? Yesterday? They don't have to be end-of-the-year-family-newsletter worthy. It's the small acts of bravery you do daily that make for living a gutsy life. What was going through your mind in those brave moments that helped you show up?

> **"It's the small acts of bravery you do daily that make for living a gutsy life."**

This idea of creating a positive script for ourselves is important. And it's not only important in times of big change in our lives; it's important *always*. No matter what is going on in life, having quick access to the positive script is vitally important. It's kind of like getting VIP tickets at Disneyland, only you aren't getting quick access to a roller coaster at a theme park—you are getting quick access to a way of grounding yourself and swifter entry to being brave.

The first step to creating a new script is to recognize and step out of the counterproductive old script.

Think of Elphaba's character in the musical *Wicked*, for example. The song "Defying Gravity" is so moving because it is the moment when she stops being defined by the script she has fed herself for years and finally steps into a more authentic one, where she gets to live the life *she* defines. In this powerful song (one of my favorites because it resonates so deeply!), she sings about how something is different, changed, about her. She's done letting other people tell her who she is and what she can be. She's going to start to learn to listen and trust in her inner wisdom and sense of knowing and take a risk so that she can live her life on her own terms.

For those of you not familiar with *Wicked*, this is the point in the show when Elphaba (the Wicked Witch) tosses aside scripts that kept her chained to an unhappy life and bravely takes up a new script to finally live a truer life. It's so beautiful, even more so because of the word *try*. She isn't sure of the outcome—we never are—but she is willing to *try* so that she may live a more authentic life.

Knock, Knock. Who's There? Me!

There is nothing quite as exhilarating as meeting yourself for the first time—stepping into who you know, deep inside your soul, you were meant to be. Even if some of what you acquaint yourself with might be painful or difficult. It is a moment of arrival, of possibility.

In my work, I treat many people who have anxiety. I have come across (at least) two types of phases people can find themselves in as they are dealing with their anxiety: those who are at a point in their life where they can take an honest look at what they are dealing with and those who are still too afraid to acknowledge that they are in extreme distress. Talking about anxiety inevitability brings up that anxiety, and not everyone is in a place where they are ready to do that hard and scary work.

This second group of people pull at my heartstrings; they are not at a place yet where they feel strong or equipped enough to acknowledge their suffering. They are operating from a false premise that they are protecting themselves by not facing their anxious thinking. They feel that their issue is too big and too scary and that they won't be able to handle it, and they stay wedded to their suffering. And there is a reason they are doing this: they are not cowardly or weak. They are so afraid to feel their anxiety because of the havoc it's brought into their lives. Facing your anxiety is one of the bravest and hardest things a person can do.

However, when we don't acknowledge areas of pain in our lives, the areas of pain gain weight, complexity, and hardship. Avoidance turns pain and suffering into even more pain and suffering because then not only are we dealing with anxiety, but we have also limited our existence so much and let go of many of our personal values because we are afraid of being swallowed by it.

When we believe that we aren't strong enough to take an honest look at what we are dealing with, healing can't happen, and our suffering deepens.

But when we can look at our reflections in the mirror and gently and compassionately say, "So this is what it feels like to have anxiety; these feelings are part of my experience right now, and what am I going to do?," we are able to take back control of our lives and figure out a way through these disabling feelings.

I'll never forget the work I did with Joey, a boy in ninth grade. He had debilitating social anxiety, to the point where he stopped going to school or doing any activities out of the house. When I first met him, I had to go greet him in his mother's car and do a mini session from there. He was too anxious to go through the waiting room and into my office.

We did good work together for a while. He eventually was able to make his way to my office for appointments. Indirectly (we were building up to talking about it more directly, but weren't quite there yet), we discussed his anxiety and the role it played in his life. Joey learned and developed some skills to better manage its draining effects. And then, one ill-fated session, we took on Joey's anxiety in a more direct way. We discussed what it felt like to acknowledge to himself that he grappled with anxiety. We discussed doing an exercise where he would practice saying out loud that he struggled with anxiety in an empowered way, where he would be able to understand that these were just words and anxiety just a feeling, and where he would learn to create some distance between himself and his anxiety. By saying these words out loud, the hope was to unidentify with the anxiety and take back his personhood. (This is a cognitive behavioral technique, where one says out loud that which they fear as a means to take back power and realize that they are not wedded to the worry.)

Although in the moment, Joey seemed strengthened by this intervention, sadly this was the last session I would have with him. I received a cryptic message from his mother, stating that it "just felt like too much" for Joey and that he needed to take a break from therapy. Joey's mother didn't respond to my offers to help Joey work through what came up for him that day. That was the end of our therapeutic relationship.

As mentioned earlier in this book, I often discuss with clients the idea of a "function within the dysfunction." That is, there are usually a whole host of reasons why we cling to unhealthy habits, scripts, and ways of being. They serve us in some respects. They may be keeping us feeling safe, protecting us from taking on the discomfort of finding a new relationship to the world, or allowing us to keep avoiding the sources of the pain.

It takes guts to step outside the story you or other people have created for you and face the hard thing. It takes bravery to step into a manuscript that the you of today—the you who knows or who is learning what you need—writes. In creating your own *brave script*, you must first allow yourself to step outside of those old scripts, old ways of thinking and believing, the ones that don't work for you anymore.

> "It takes guts to step outside the story you or other people have created for you and face the hard thing."

We all have scripts we have outgrown—scripts that have been largely shaped by other people or what we believe other people see in us. It is funny for me, as I write this book, to reflect on old scripts I had for myself that don't work anymore today.

One such narrative is *I am not a good writer.*

I'm not saying I think I am the most talented and prolific writer, but in high school, I was the epitome of a perfectionistic and high achiever. I received nearly perfect grades and rarely missed a day of school (one year I even got an award for perfect attendance—don't try this at home, kids). But my perfection streak ended with high school English. I had the same English teacher for three out of four years in high school and, no matter how hard I tried, how much I edited my work, I couldn't get an *A*.

My conclusion was that I must not be a very good writer. I have vague memories of being told something like that by my English teacher as well.

So that was that: I tried, I couldn't seem to pull off *As* on my writing assignments, and so concluded English was obviously not my strong suit. That became my script: I could excel at other subjects, but not English, because it just wasn't my *thing*.

Enter college. I took, with low expectations, an English class as a necessary prerequisite. It was to be a "one and done" relationship for me. And then, I fell in love with English and writing. I loved reading, writing, and analyzing so much I took extra English literature classes and was one class short of being an English minor on top of my psychology major. And I did well; I got good grades and was (finally) being told that my writing was good.

I was so surprised in the beginning because I was coming out of four formative years holding a strong belief that I *wasn't* a strong writer. But now I learned that I was capable of writing well.

I am thankful that I had those teachers and those experiences in college to prove that old belief wrong. I have a sneaking feeling that if I hadn't had the opportunity to challenge those beliefs, there is the possibility I wouldn't have gone on for my PhD in psychology, let alone write this book.

We all have old scripts—either ones that are no longer true or were *never* true.

These scripts can rear their heads in any dimension of life. They can revolve around more surface issues, such as what kind of driver you are, or hit at more core aspects of you: your spirituality, your inherent self-worth, your ability to love and be in a relationship, and so on.

What are some scripts you are holding on to that don't serve you? Can you try on a new, more empowering script? View it as an experiment—like trying on a new hat. You may find it emboldening and lightening.

In my own spiritual journey, I have had to step outside of old spiritual scripts that weren't working for me anymore.

I have had to examine and rewrite my running script about some of the Jewish holidays. Most of the holidays I love naturally: they are fun, they are cozy, and I have many positive memories of celebrating them year after year. However, there is one holiday that I am not fond of, even though it is happy and joyous: Purim. I always felt it was more of a man's holiday, and because of this sentiment, I have fewer positive memories with this one.

(For those of you who may not be familiar with the holiday, Purim is an early spring celebratory holiday marking the defeat of a wicked Persian ruler who wanted to eliminate all the Jews. Today, Jewish people celebrate it by dressing up, delivering food baskets, spending time in synagogue, and having a festive meal with family and friends.)

A couple of Purims ago, I had an epiphany—maybe I don't have to dislike Purim anymore. Maybe this is an old story that I am telling myself, and it no longer has to be true. I can find new, more meaningful ways of connecting with the holiday. As a mother, I decided to try to view this holiday from an entirely fresh angle—from that of my children—which really helped me find a new joy in it, a new happiness in celebrating it with my family. One way to challenge an old script is to approach the scenario or experience by pretending to have just discovered something new, something we don't have prior attachments to or notions about. Is there something in your life with which you can bring fresh perspective?

Old scripts can be incredibly self-limiting and the things that hold us back from greater fulfillment in life.

> "Our power stems from what we tell ourselves, what we believe we are capable of."

But positive, self-affirming scripts push us forward to live a life of greatness and challenge. We have more say than most of us know about what we can accomplish in our lives. And a lot of our power stems from what we tell ourselves, what we believe we are capable of.

> "When we believe in possibilities, we are more likely to attempt them."

These new helpful scripts open up doors of possibility. They allow us to take risks in how we live and what we allow ourselves to try. When we believe in possibilities, we are more likely to attempt them.

These positive scripts—they help us be brave.

Take a Look at Your Old (Defunct) Scripts

What are some old, pesky scripts you tell yourself? Take time to write them down. Evaluate the nature of them: Are they working for you? Are they true? For the ones that aren't working, do you want them to dictate how you live the rest of your life? Remind yourself that all of these scripts come from one past experience or another, and we can't let the past define us. It is time to focus on the present—and the future. You get to decide what you will tell yourself, what you will do with the unhelpful thoughts, and what you choose to believe about yourself in the next moment and in all the tomorrows.

> **"You get to decide what you will tell yourself, what you will do with the unhelpful thoughts, and what you choose to believe about yourself in the next moment and in all the tomorrows."**

One script I use that helps me live my life bravely is "I am perseverant. I will do what it takes to get it done." This is what helps me persevere, even when I get rejections and the road ahead is not clear and very bumpy. It's why you are holding this book in your hand (publishing a book is not for the tender hearted! It takes lots of "nos" to get the "yes").

Underline the scripts that serve you and help you live a passionate and fulfilling life. Cross out the ones that are past their expiration date and need to get thrown out. Create new ones that will serve you well on this journey of living a fulfilling life of self-discovery! We don't necessarily get to choose all of what we think (all kinds of thoughts will inevitably pop up in our wonderful minds), but we sure as hell get to choose what to do with our thoughts.

You don't have to have all the evidence for these new, emboldening scripts yet. When we say and believe empowering things about ourselves and our potential, we engage our self-fulfilling prophecy mechanism. This means, we are more likely to take actions in line with our beliefs and stretch ourselves in meaningful ways, thus confirming the validity of these newer, empowering scripts, and reinforcing them.

Say this:

*It's about time I learned to live a life free of years-old scripts
that just don't work for me right now.*

*I deserve to live the rest of my life coming back to scripts of
strength and hopefulness.*

*When an old script comes up, I will welcome it in like an old
friend, one with whom I have a lot of shared history.*

*I will honor it by looking at it and acknowledging it. Then I
will honor myself by letting it go.*

7

Feeling Braver in Our Relationships

We are all just people.

Dealing with (Perceived) Judgment

One outdated script that I have had to work a lot on is the worry script of being judged by other people—and not even necessarily people very close to me.

At different points in my life, in relation to fears I have had about finding acceptance from others, I have found my mind producing variations of the same fun script, which sounds something like: *What will other people think about me? What if an idea I have is really no good and is not received well? I will feel inept.*

For many of my clients, fear of judgment is one of their biggest barriers to well-being: the college freshman who didn't speak up for herself when things were going very wrong with her roommate, the young woman who told close family she was having trouble with infertility when really she was ashamed to admit she wasn't ready for a baby, the teenage girl who didn't want to tell her parents she was suicidal for fear of their judgment, or the teenage boy who wouldn't tell his mother he was depressed and was attempting to deal with it on his own.

"We are all just people."

One script that has helped me face my fear of judgment with bravery is *We are all just people*—all of us, even my superiors and elders and rabbis and parents.

We are all just people who are more alike than we are different. Each of us is struggling and living with our unique set of circumstances to the best of our abilities. No better, no worse, just different. In fact, you share 99.9 percent of your DNA with every other human.[1]

Framing interactions with others this way helps with grounding and creating an awareness that we are all on the same playing field. No one is better than anyone else. We were born equal, after all. Even someone who intimidates me because of their success—they are also just a person. Like me. There is something connecting and beautiful and equalizing about noticing our shared humanity.

This truth, of equal and inherent human self-worth, sadly gets muddled because of legitimate inequalities that do exist in our culture. These injustices might make it *seem* that a person's privilege is tied to their worth. Of course, this couldn't be farther from the truth. Every single one of us has the same inherent value, despite societal inequalities that exist and might make it feel otherwise. There is nothing that increases one human's worth over another's. Sadly, there is so much work still needed to be done to make sure we are all really at the same playing field.

When I was breaking from some of the traditional religious rules of my childhood and my early adult years, I had to remind myself that *we are all just people* often. In the beginning of my transformation, I was afraid of what the rabbis who had known me when I was conforming to the norms of our Orthodox Jewish community would think if they saw me wearing pants or with my hair uncovered. Allowing myself to appear in public as is—in the capacity that felt right for me, which was not in line with how people from my past expected me to look—felt scary.

I remember standing in line at the kosher deli of the local supermarket and seeing a rabbi of our small town approaching the deli counter. Normally this would be no cause for stress or concern for me, but on this particular day, watching him approach was a significant cause of anxiety. I so badly wanted to bolt. Why? I was wearing *jeans*. It was one of the first times I had worn pants in public, let alone jeans (which felt like a greater break from tradition), and I hadn't yet bumped into members of my community who had known me when I was strictly a skirt-wearing lady.

This is what went through my head in that moment: *If I run now, in the other direction, I think I'll get away before he sees me.*

My impulse was to run and get the hell out of there. Maybe you've had a similar experience. I almost did run; it would have been easier and saved me from the feelings of my own shame and disgrace. I could have evaded those feelings by avoiding opening myself up to the possible judgment—including the wonderfully creative array of judgments my own mind was producing.

However—and I am grateful I made this choice—I decided to keep my feet firmly planted where they were and embrace my vulnerability. I believe my mindfulness training helped me do that and allowed me to hold what was unfolding for me and stay grounded in the moment. I said my hello, briefly noticed I was feeling quite uncomfortable, and went on my way.

Allowing myself to be brave in this way became a template for doing more of the same. Instead of shying away from people or situations in which I may have felt shame or discomfort around, I made myself stay present and open myself up to these experiences as teachable moments.

Now, this wasn't *every* time. There were some moments where I legitimately steered myself in a different direction than what I had intended (in the grocery store, no less!) so as to not bump into someone because of the shame I felt and the fear of judgment. But there were many other moments where I went to an event wearing pants or with my hair uncovered because that's what felt true to me. And I did it with the experience of feeling self-conscious and anxious.

I felt self-conscious and anxious, but I also felt gutsy.

It was not easy for me to choose a different lifestyle than what was laid out for me. It took courage, independence, and decisiveness—all things that didn't often come naturally to me. I am proud and grateful for the way I have navigated this journey so far.

Fear of judgment shows up in our professional lives as well. I can't be the only one to have had the following experience: You are in a room of highly educated people for an event with a speaker, and when the speaker says, "Raise your hand if you don't know what [X] is?," no one else raises their hand and you wonder why you are the only dummy in the room. Or the speaker takes your expertise for granted, saying something like (for me, specifically, in this example), "You're a psychologist, so you must know what *[Y]* is." It takes bravery to say, "Actually I don't. Can you please let me know what that is?"

Being real, really, truly showing up for ourselves and letting other people in on our less-than-perfect composition, takes bravery. And it is such a gift to the world. And to ourselves.

> *"Bravery* is showing up for the real you who lives within, regardless of what your conscious and thinking mind might be telling you."

Bravery is showing up for the real you who lives within, regardless of what your conscious and thinking mind might be telling you.

It takes guts to recraft your story and step outside of old storylines that don't fit anymore. But it is a crucial step in forging a new path forward.

Find Your Inner Chutzpah

Maybe this interaction sounds familiar to you:

What movie do you want to watch? "Oh, I'm easy to please—whatever movie you had in mind."

Or in response to that friend who canceled at the last minute (three times in a row) when we had plans with each other, you say, "No worries! Next time!"

So many of us make choices to avoid perceived confrontation and limit setting. This is particularly true for those of us who have had difficult upbringings where we weren't noticed very much. We will put a smile on our faces and learn to stifle our feelings in order to be liked, to feel more certain about ourselves. To be perceived as a nice person.

Aside from our childhoods, this trait of being agreeable is also much more common among women than men. Some psychologists hypothesize that this trait of agreeableness is at the root of the gender-wage inequality. Some psychologists say that women are scientifically shown to be more agreeable (read: people pleasers) than men; therefore, men are less inhibited in asking for what they want than women are.

To take another example: women scientists author 21 percent fewer invited commentaries in medical journals than men,[2] and women are underrepresented as first authors of original research in high-impact general medical journals. This was looked at over a period of twenty years.[3] Data shows us that, for some reason, women are living more in the shadows than men.

So why are many of us women too agreeable and find it hard to set limits?

I believe the answer to this lies in female societal expectations, as well as family values.

In many families, we are taught to be nonconfrontational and agreeable. We have family members who model this behavior, taking on the role of the martyr. The blueprint ends up being give and give of yourself, without giving *to* yourself, until you are depleted and resentful of all you did.

Confronting someone with hurt feelings or even setting limits can be looked down on and labeled as selfish. If we have trouble setting or enforcing our own boundaries, a good first question to ask ourselves is how were boundaries treated in our family of origin? If there was boundary trouble there, then there is a good chance this is something you struggle with as an adult. I remember venting to someone I looked up to about some legitimate wrong that had been directed at me and saying, "And I didn't say anything to her about it" as a way of lamenting my meekness. And this person's response was "Wow, Leah, it is so good you can be quiet like that." How many of you received similar messaging? If we receive messages that reinforce our quietness—and not our voices—we often will develop complex feelings toward our right to self-advocate and practice assertive communication.

To this day it is hard for me to speak up and respect my gut when someone has wronged me. But I am aware of it, and I am getting better at speaking up when something feels wrong. And let me tell you, the more and more I do it, the easier it gets—and it feels *so* good.

Getting in touch with your inner chutzpah means if there is something going on—if you have been hurt, let down, or taken advantage of—*say something.*

Be brave in how you relate to others by setting boundaries. In other words, *speak up, girl, and don't worry too much about what other people might think.*

> "Getting in touch with your inner chutzpah means if there is something going on—if you have been hurt, let down, or taken advantage of—*say something*."

I am embarrassed over how many times I *didn't* say something, whether it was paying more than I had initially agreed to or even just apologizing to appease someone over something I didn't do. Over time, I have learned to speak up more and more. It is empowering to let go of the belief that we have to be agreeable at all times and allow ourselves to say something. It is so emboldening to find your voice.

This doesn't mean we need to air every grievance. It also doesn't mean we should be unskillful in how we communicate about the infraction. But it does mean that if something is bothering you, you should find a way to address it. That might mean intentionally accepting what happened or deciding to say something about it, but don't just ignore it. Be true to yourself and listen to your inner wisdom, the part of you that *knows*.

Not only does addressing how you are feeling lighten your load, it is a way of affirming that you and your needs are *important*. Far more important than some old flawed beliefs that have to do with needing everyone around you to like you all the time.

Several years back, I put together a volunteer committee. One person in the group, who I had a burgeoning friendship with, repeatedly didn't respond to texts, would offer to do things and then not follow through, and was all around frustrating to deal with. Old me would have felt frustrated, probably vented to a friend and my husband, and continued putting on a big smile like nothing was bothering me.

I would get a text in the middle of a meeting—"I'm so sorry I didn't see there was a meeting until just now"—and my old answer would have been "No worries! We miss you!"

This old script would cause resentment to stew and fester inside of me and even lead me to behaviors I don't want to embody—like gossiping behind this friend's back.

So I approached her (I like this word better than confronted—it makes it feel more palatable for people who are afraid of confrontation). I was nice, probably still *too* nice, but I didn't whitewash it away. I think this surprised her, and our friendship took a hit.

But you know what? I felt awesome. I felt confident. I felt like I had more control over my life and was able to enjoy more authentic connections with people. And, in this case, our friendship rebounded.

Another time I was at a retreat, and the women on the other side of the paper-thin wall would make phone calls late at night—interfering with my ability to sleep when I had to wake up at 5:00 a.m. the next morning. In the past, I may have ignored it (okay, I definitely would not have said anything)—or acted out in a passive aggressive way. However, I made a different choice this time. I walked out of my room, politely knocked on her door, and took in her surprised face as I asked her to please not make phone calls from her room because I was trying to sleep and it was late. She was annoyed with me, sure, and said something to that effect, but she hung up the phone, and I felt both energized and better rested.

It just doesn't feel good to put that smile on your face and inwardly resent the people around you. It is not good or healthy to carry that around. Even if it means letting go of some relationships. Because the ones that are left will be real and deeper.

And let yourself be surprised by your relationships. I have set limits or spoken up, fully expecting the relationship to suffer as a result. And you know what? It didn't.

Most often, in fact, bringing up the difficult conversation was respected, and it encouraged more authenticity in the friendship. It was hard to have certain conversations, yes, and maybe I was not fully understood or heard at all times; however, standing my ground and asserting what was truly important to me enriched my relationships and made *me* feel lighter and more confident.

Speaking up for ourselves is an act of self-compassion. By not putting up with circumstances that are unhealthy and

> "Speaking up for ourselves is an act of self-compassion."

eat away at us, we make more space for our own well-being and growth.

But even those of us *without* little versions of ourselves telling us we must not disappoint people tend to not be completely honest with our feelings, even with those closest to us. And we have to wonder why? Why do we find it so hard to voice our truths? What are we afraid of, really?

I am always in awe of the women I know who are not afraid to speak their minds if something or someone is bothering them. How did they get to be that way? These women were raised to be confident with their emotions and needs (or did the work themselves) and allow themselves to put them out there, even with the risk that they will ruffle some feathers because they know they can handle the consequences. Their worth isn't tied to other people's opinions of them, and they don't overthink things.

Therefore, I am proposing to get in touch with the part of you that knows what you need and can recognize when someone has crossed a line. That part of you also knows when an issue is important enough for you to say something about it. Listen to this piece of your own wisdom and act on it. By doing so, you are teaching yourself a lesson in self-worth: you being good or kind is not dependent purely on how others view you. It is a kindness and a gift—offering those closest to us deep authenticity and vulnerability. If a good friend forgot your birthday, say something—gently, kindly—and notice how you feel afterward. Notice how your relationships evolve and deepen. Notice which relationships can sustain that kind of openness and which ones cannot.

Not all relationships can sustain that kind of openness, and that is okay. There are different kinds of relationships. The closer, more central ones are the ones we especially want to bring our most authentic selves to.

Answer these questions for yourself:

How are you with needing to please other people?
How are you with speaking up for yourself and setting limits?
Can you think of a real-life role model, someone you know
    who has mastered the art of being comfortable in their
    own skin? What can you "borrow" from them and make
    your own?
Are there any old resentments you are holding on to that you
    can speak up about?
How can you start, today, practicing more assertiveness and
    confidence with how you conduct yourself?

Sometimes, the answer to this lies in how we carry ourselves: when you choose to have a difficult conversation, try doing so with a dignified posture, a firm tone, and eye contact. Notice your tendency to apologize or make excuses, and try, instead, being more direct with your message.

Slow Down

At one meditation retreat, I had a few moments to chat with the leader one on one. I'm a fast talker by nature (thank you, New York upbringing!), but mixing that with my eagerness, I wound up trying to cram too many thoughts into the few moments I had with him. Partway into our conversation, he looked at me, put his hand up, and then told me, quite bluntly, to "slow down." That pretty much stopped me in my tracks, and I didn't finish what I wanted to say. At the time, it hurt (and was embarrassing!) to hear this, but he was totally right: I was speaking way too quickly; even my brain was having a hard time catching up with the jumble of words falling out of my mouth.

This experience got me thinking. How deliberate are we when talking with others? Maybe we can slow it down a notch or two and be more thoughtful in our speech, allow ourselves to take time to collect our thoughts, and push back against the fast pace of the world around us. We can also start to pay attention to other nonverbal ways of communicating, like eye contact. When we slow down, we are more able to take in the other human before us and meaningfully connect with them.

There is a beautiful mindfulness practice called "relational dharma" or "insight dialogue" where we focus our attention on the person we are with or the energy that is being created in the space between two people. The goal is to observe the other—notice *their* breathing or the way they smile or (all!) the colors of their eyes or how the light reflects off the highlights in their hair—and balance this awareness of what's happening outside us in the other person with an internal awareness of our own bodies.

Using this practice when we are communicating with others enhances a genuine connection with them. Because if we're honest, so often we are thinking about something not related to what the other person is saying while they are talking. Or prepping a response to what they are saying. Doing this practice helps us get out of our heads and into the moment we are sharing with this other individual.

I find myself practicing this in my therapeutic work: taking my time to formulate a thought and making meaningful eye contact. Noticing the tendency to look away as we think of something to say (it's an interesting habit many of us do). Many of my clients express some embarrassment when a thought doesn't come out right or it is taking them longer than they think is socially appropriate to get a thought out, or they think they are being confusing in some way. They apologize for it or make excuses. *I don't know why I can't talk today.* I often reply with something reassuring and ask them why they feel the need to apologize.

I think of one young man I treated in therapy who apologized multiple times every session for stumbling over words or "not knowing what to say." We have explored how at the root of these apologies is some lack of trust, in himself, as well as in me (for being able to hold space with him for whatever might be arising). It is also a form of avoidance of uncomfortable feelings that arise in session: his discomfort with silence, and with not knowing.

Let's all slow it down. Give ourselves permission to take our time. Trust ourselves. Trust the ones we are with. There is something so brave, raw, and vulnerable in allowing ourselves to do this. In fact, one study found that when people were asked to answer questions quickly and impulsively, they were more likely to respond with a socially desirable answer versus a true one.[4] When we rush ourselves, we are less authentic. Let's slow it down, allowing ourselves to be more deliberate and, thereby, more honest and connecting in our communications.

> "When we rush ourselves, we are less authentic. Let's slow it down, allowing ourselves to be more deliberate and, thereby, more honest and connecting in our communications."

Say this:

We are all just people.
Me and you and everyone in this world.
I will not let another finite person dictate how I feel
about myself. Only I will take hold of that awesome
responsibility.

8

Living Bravely with Your Body

Look at what this body can do.

I was having a lot of shoulder pain and didn't know why. A massage therapist pointed out how I would tense my shoulder and raise it toward my ear, often and without knowing it, and this was the likely culprit of my pain. I now notice more often when I am tensing that area of my body and contributing to the pain.

When we take the time to pay attention to our bodies—in a kind and gentle way—we learn a whole lot about them that we would have missed if we hadn't. I always find it amazing (in the most compassionate of ways!) how so many of us are out of touch with our bodies (like my story here) and missing the important information they are relaying to us. We are so busy *doing* life and *thinking* about life that we literally ignore what our body is telling us until the discomfort becomes too much. What starts as a whisper becomes a talk, which then becomes a scream. And *then* we pause and listen to our bodies because now that it's loud, well, it's creating too much of a disruption to our *doing* that we must attend to it.

> "When we learn to *be*—to slow down and pay attention lovingly to the physical component of our humanity—we are more likely to *hear* the whispers and *respond* to them compassionately."

But, if we slow down, listen, and check in more frequently with how our bodies are doing, we'll start to hear the quiet talking and murmurings of our body and attend to what it needs, hopefully before it gets too loud. This is one of the benefits of learning how to be a human *being* in addition to a human *doing*. When we learn to *be*—to slow down and pay attention lovingly to the physical component of our humanity—we are more likely to *hear* the whispers and *respond* to them compassionately.

Beyond the personal stories held in our bodies, there is a cultural story to be told as well. As women, we often find that our bodies can be the source of loaded and heavy conversations. Messages we have heard from society, family, and our own minds about our bodies are too frequently destructive, inaccurate, and harmful. How many of us have experienced some sort of harassment, abuse, or toxicity in relationship to our female body from strangers or even people we know?

Just in picking up a magazine—or watching a TV show—we are bombarded by implicit and explicit messages about the female body. Even my eleven-year-old son turned to me recently and insightfully commented as we were browsing for a movie to watch, "Why are all the covers of all these movies of women? In some of them, they are barely even in the movie!" Out of the mouths of children, friends. Women are hypersexualized in our culture to such a degree that if we weren't so desensitized to it, we might feel a stronger sense of injustice. And the degree to which this messaging affects women globally, compared to the limited extent to which it is addressed, is really not okay.

Body shaming, ageism, sexual harassment, rape, abuse—these are things that women contend with throughout their lives. Even certain mental illnesses—such as the whole classification of eating disorders, which are diagnosed mostly in women—are often expressions of self-loathing and control directed at our own bodies.

We need to talk more with each other about how we feel about our bodies, process the trauma and rage, and build each other up.

One way we can develop healthier relationships with our bodies is learning to bring attention and care for what is actually transpiring inside them. This can lend itself to both gratitude and taking better care of our precious homes. It's amazing how many of us are walking around with unaddressed pain and discomfort, maybe even suffering, much of which we aren't even fully aware of.

A friend of mine recently shared that she had been having hip pain for *two years*. She had ignored it, thought it would go away on its own, and went about her life. She finally made an appointment with a chiropractor and in one thirty-minute session, her pain was relieved. *Thirty minutes. Two years.* Wow. Creating an awareness of the pain and doing something about it were all it took to address and alleviate her pain.

Take this moment to briefly scan your body. Do you feel any tension or pain that you have been carrying around with you and have not addressed? Is there some way to release the tension, right now? If it's a more complex issue, can you commit to acting to help yourself? It's remarkable how many of us ignore our aches. Because they are not intolerable, and we are not in crisis, we just take them for granted and carry on.

At one point while I was in labor with my first child, I called in a nurse, frantic that I was losing sensation in my hands. I thought there was something very wrong, and my hands were becoming paralyzed. The nurse held up my hands for me to see how I was clenching my fists so hard (from the labor pains) that I was cutting off circulation. I even had nail prints inside the palms of my hands because I was scrunching them so tight. I had no awareness that I was doing this, and it's something I've thought of often in cultivating greater awareness of my body, especially in times of distress.

Of course, this story is a unique circumstance because I *was in labor* at the time and birthing pains are, well, pains. And yet if we begin this work by bringing awareness to our bodies in easier, calmer moments, we can reinforce the capacity to be with ourselves and our experience when it may be much harder to be present for the sensations in our bodies.

> **"We can learn to practice kindness and acceptance with our bodies, in whatever state they are in."**

For many of us, our bodies can be one of our biggest sources of pain. But we can learn to practice kindness and acceptance with our bodies, in whatever state they are in. Knowing that our bodies, as with our identities discussed in earlier chapters, are constantly changing.

Please note: Not all pain is equal, and the pain we carry in our bodies stems from many different causes. What I am referring to here are the typical aches and pains that come with having a human body, not people with medical conditions that cause pain. It is important to always be safe with your body and follow the guidelines of your medical advisor. Please do not try anything in this book that goes against your physician's advice or does not feel right for your body.

Exercise Mindfully and Lovingly

I'm sure we've all heard all about the psychological and physical benefits of exercise, but I'd like to take some space here to revisit how moving our bodies can help us in so many ways. I won't go into the vast scientific literature that supports and discusses the health benefits of movement (more on that in chapter 12), but I will share some of my own clinical observations. When a client comes to see me with any particular difficulty—chronic stress, anxiety, depression, you name it—I always think of dividing treatment into two different camps: preventative strategies, or the things we can do to put our best foot forward, so to speak, to keep ourselves mentally well, and treatment interventions, or skills we can learn to address the particular area of discomfort when it arises.

Exercise falls easily into both camps: it is something we can and should build into our day-to-day routine to keep ourselves well and prevent the buildup of too much stress. *And* it is something that can be so helpful as part of a treatment plan. As basic, easy, and nonclinical as it sounds, moving our bodies is crucial to feeling well.

I will often recommend to individuals coming in for therapy to make sure they are moving their bodies in some way every day, ideally combining movement with time spent outside (another huge thing for our mental wellness) or even combining movement with socializing by identifying a workout buddy, someone to move with and keep us accountable in our pursuit of health.

If movement is not your favorite thing, pairing it with something more pleasurable like listening to a great audiobook or some good music can aid you in building this habit.

I had a mental shift a few years ago. At that first pivotal meditation retreat I've written about in earlier chapters, while practicing yoga, the retreat leader said something that may sound small but created a huge shift in how I related to my body, particularly in moments of exercise-induced discomfort.

> **"Let's see what this body can do."**

He said, "Let's see what this body can do."

These are words I repeat to myself when I am engaged in a particularly difficult exercise routine. When I notice myself getting stuck in my head and having thoughts of *I hate this!* or *Why did I do this?* or *Maybe I should surreptitiously sneak out of this yoga class while everyone is doing downward dog and won't notice me putting my mat away and leaving.*

I shift out of that thinking and instead repeat this simple phrase to myself: "Let's see what this body can do." And it helps me get out of my head and into my own body. I feel the stretch, I feel the burn; sometimes those sensations inform me to stop, and sometimes they inform me as to what my body can tolerate. These words encourage me to apply a gentleness to how I move and stretch that make movement more enjoyable and, ultimately, doable (as a side note: Did you know that doing yoga is associated with less depression and anxiety?).[1]

I use this phrase as I run as well. Running, to a large degree, is about stretching the mind's ability to dig deep and sustain discomfort. Of course, it helps and is useful to build up stamina to run better, but even with that, there always comes a point in any run when we just have to dig deep and get over the mental hurdle of wanting to stop and walk. When this happens to me, in most every run I go on, I come back to this phrase: *let's see what this body can do*. It opens up the experience to kind curiosity and gently pushing limits in a healthy way, and it often gets me to keep going. And sometimes, it informs me to slow down and walk.

Please note, this is not permission to be harsh with your body or push it to do something that it does not want to do, which may be harmful or lead to injury. "Let's see what this body can do" has to do with mindset and adopting a more connected and curious relationship with our bodies. The outcome of this mindset might either be choosing to sink in to the challenge of the moment or listening to your body's limits and choosing to stop or adapt an exercise or movement. These are equally important responses.

The times when we choose to get out of our heads and challenge ourselves physically, walking right up to the self-limiting beliefs you have about your body and pushing through them, can be pretty amazing. Again, this is different from testing our bodies' limits in a harsh, aggressive way. This is more about noticing the thoughts our mind has created about what our body can or cannot do and not allowing ourselves to follow them blindly. We can learn instead to be curious and open to questioning their veracity. When we do this, in the gentlest of ways, and realize that previously we were being led around by faulty beliefs, it is actually quite exhilarating. And surprising. It adds an adventuresome spirit to how we live.

One of my favorite yoga teachers would say, "Notice how much easier it is to be with your body as it rests, as opposed to holding (a difficult position)." Just noticing the difference between experiences can be profound: by paying attention to our different thoughts about each of these experiences, we can begin to change how we are with ourselves in those moments when we are stretching our bodies.

I have never been flexible, even as a very young child. I was the girl who couldn't touch her toes or do a cartwheel, let alone the splits. I practiced—I wanted to be able to do these physical feats so badly—but eventually I gave up, telling myself I simply did not have a body cut out to stretch itself that way.

So when I started doing yoga more regularly several years ago and the teacher had us wrap our arms backward around our body, I didn't even try. I had told myself, long ago, that *my body is not flexible.* Somewhere, deep inside of me, *I just knew* I couldn't do it.

Until I did it (after several classes of building up this ability).

The thrill of doing something I had told myself for years that I couldn't do was amazing. I won't forget it. Nor will I forget the sensation of my fingers clasping behind me in this pose I had long thought impossible for my body.

And just like that, the limiting belief is shattered.

More recently, I had another physical high. When I was eight, I had a severe bike accident where I totaled a friend's bike and seriously cut up my knees, one elbow, and part of my chin. I told myself I was done with bike riding. I could get along just fine without ever having to go on a bike again, thank you very much. But then, years later on a family vacation, I was getting left behind, while my family went on magnificent bike rides without me—even my four-year-old. *That's it*, I told myself. *I am getting back on the bike.*

Feeling quite anxious, I went to the bike rental shop and told the young clerk that I needed to rent a bike, murmuring that I hadn't been on one in a very long time. I didn't specify how long, but I was painfully aware—twenty-eight years.

He said, "No problem" and asked me to try out a bike to see if it fit well. It was actually quite embarrassing, wobbling around on that bike for all to see and barely even able to get my feet to pedal. I didn't think he would lend me the bike after witnessing my basically nonexistent biking skills. But after reassuring him I would practice in front of the house, he rented me the bike, and I wobbled—er, *biked*—away.

I practiced and practiced and almost fell several times. I reminded myself to breathe and stay present over and over, because I noticed every time I got stuck in the anxiety and memories of my scary bike fall, I would almost crash the bike.

Over the course of the afternoon, I retaught myself to ride a bike. I honestly didn't think I would ever ride again. It was exhilarating and empowering and wonderful.

This is the power of recognizing, paying attention to, and deciding what to do with the limiting beliefs we have about our physical capabilities. So much of the time these beliefs are based on fear, anxiety, and untruths. If we can free our mind of these shackles, we can overcome more than what we thought was possible—or at least learn to live more intentionally about what we are choosing to apply ourselves to and challenge ourselves by.

It is like looking down a hallway of closed doors you had always assumed were locked and off-limits only to realize all you had to do was try the nob and the door would open.

Sometimes it's slow, and sometimes it's hard. But we can get it opened one way or another. And the interesting thing is, after we've tried the nob and opened the door, we realize how we held both the key and the lock in our minds the whole time. It can be so, so liberating. I want to emphasize that I am not saying all people are capable of all physical things. Of course not. We all have our own very real limitations. I am saying pause, slow down, and reflect on the messages and guidance you are taking from your mind—without question—and start to intentionally choose in (or out) of what your mind is telling you. (You might not be interested in getting back on the bike! And that is okay.)

I've had the experience a few times after climbing over a perceived mountain, some challenge or activity my mind was telling me would be über-scary—whatever it was—and looking behind me to see it was really a mountain composed of mist. Only my mind interpreted the mist as a mountain, and all I had to do was take the steps to walk through it.

I remember the exact moment when this thought about the misty mountain came to me. I had wanted to develop a more public platform for a long time and connect with a larger audience, but I was afraid. Of failure. Of judgment. Of feeling shame. I had made several videos with messages I wanted to share with world, but they lived quietly on the hard drive of my old Mac. In my mind, I was never going to publish any of those videos. I made the videos for fun, and actually publishing them felt like a pipe dream.

However, I changed my relationship with that fear one memorable morning. I was part of a small women's group

> "It's choosing to make those *small* gutsy choices that set us up on a path of bravery and living a more authentic life."

that felt safe and supportive and had a WhatsApp group. That morning, I had filmed a video with an idea and didn't post it, as per my usual. This morning was different, though. I embraced a new mindset, one of adventure and openness to risk and new possibility. I made the video, took a deep breath, and—boop—posted it. It was a small step on the outside, but it felt really quite huge for me. It was less about what I had actually done (posted creative content to my WhatsApp group) and more about the process of what I had just taught myself experientially: how fear-based thoughts blow things up in our minds and how left attended become the drivers of our life. When we get ourselves to do the thing, we realize it isn't as hard as we thought or imagined it to be. Pressing the send button felt liberating, freeing, and lightening—and terrifying. It's choosing to make those *small* gutsy choices that set us up on a path of bravery and living a more authentic life. I remember going into Fred Meyer shortly after I had hit send feeling like a superstar because I had just moved aside thoughts that were holding me back from doing something I really wanted to do.

This is not to say that some goals aren't really difficult—many of the challenges we face in life can be *very* difficult. And that is okay. If we can learn to stay compassionately present with ourselves in the middle of the pursuit of our goals and the thoughts that pop up for us around moving forward with them, without getting swept away by the anxiety of the *what ifs*, we can push through more than we think. And along the way, we flex and build the muscles of perseverance, presence, gentleness, and kindness to ourselves that is an exhilarating adjunct to life.

An incredible book called *The Brain That Changes Itself: Stories of Personal Triumph from the Frontiers of Brain Science*, written by Norman Doidge, is about neuroplasticity—the ability the brain has to transform and regain abilities once thought impossible. It is an incredible read about what we are capable of with hard work and perseverance at the neurobiological level.

Again, many times when I have been in a yoga class or running on the treadmill, the absolute right decision was to not push myself because the exercise wasn't right for my body at the time or running any more would have been unhealthy for me. This is about the subjective balance and relationship you have with your body: looking honestly at limiting thoughts and connecting with the powerful force your body is—in whatever condition it is in—and always, *always* treating your body with kindness first.

Do What You Love

For much of my life, exercise—in whatever form—was always a chore. Something I had to endure with all-too-often intense duress. I would look at the clock as the seconds ticked away ever so slowly, and I couldn't wait for the designated time to end. Sometimes it was running for thirty minutes, and sometimes it was burning three hundred calories. Whatever it was, I didn't like it. Not a bit.

Is this your experience with exercising as well? It is something you know you are supposed to do to take care of yourself, but you can't seem to find a method of physical activity that you actually like or *want* to do?

I went through a popular 30-day YouTube fitness program years ago. It was rigorous and intense, and I hated every single second of it—and I also injured my knees to the point where it hurt to walk. No matter—I kept on going, despite the pain.

I'm sure there are a lot of people out there (please, come talk to me!) who love those kinds of super rigorous and challenging workouts. I have a dear friend who thrives on the challenge in completing difficult workout classes. I made the mistake of joining her in an advanced-level (or what felt advanced to me!) weight-lifting group fitness class. I think I was able to make it through maybe five minutes of that class before feeling utterly exhausted. Five miserable minutes. She loved it, I hated it.

The point? There are many ways to exercise our bodies. Choose something you love—not necessarily always while it's happening (because exercising can be hard!)—but you love the feeling you get when you are done. You may not love it all the time, and there may be some times when it is more of a chore for you than others. Regardless, choose something that makes you feel strong, powerful, and alive as well as something whose process you enjoy (much of the time), keeping in mind that exercising also often takes a big dose of discipline. Sometimes we need to push ourselves to get going, knowing we will reap the reward of feeling great and empowered when we are done. Running, tennis, swimming, yoga—you name it. There are so many fun and creative ways of exercising. And while you're at it, put on some fun upbeat music, as this has been shown to make rigorous exercise seem less grueling and more enjoyable—even for people who are not very active.[2]

And most importantly, make a point of noticing how you feel when you are done. I often run and bike. Sometimes

> "There are many ways to exercise our bodies. Choose something you love—not necessarily always while it's happening (because exercising can be hard!)—but you love the feeling you get when you are done."

I love it while it's happening, but to be perfectly honest, sometimes I hate it. But no matter what, there is nothing quite like the high and sense of satisfaction I feel when I am done. It is so good for my mental health, and that is why I keep on showing up for it on the days when I don't feel like it, not for any in-the-moment passion I have for running, but for that amazing feeling I get when I am done.

So try to find movement you love—perhaps you love it while you are doing it, but most importantly, you love how you feel when you are done. Find movement that gives you lightness and confidence and satisfaction. Maybe it's walks outside or dancing. Or strength training. Or biking. Or a mix of a lot of different things.

Connect to Movement throughout the Day

It is great if we can fit in a longer workout, but sometimes finding a way to move our body lies in shorter moments throughout the day.

I started taking the stairs up to my fourth-floor office at work (most days). I'm pretty huffy by the time I get up there, especially early in the morning. But I do it because moving my body is important to me, and connecting to that value in this small way feels good.

I didn't used to take the stairs. I would look smugly at the stair takers in the morning as I waited for the elevator, thinking, *I don't want the hassle of the stairs. I'll run later. And besides—what is going up four measly flights of stairs going to do for me anyway?*

But something shifted for me. It was the shift from looking at the bigger picture and bigger goals to seeing the value in the smaller things.

It is connecting to those smaller steps that really anchors us to the people we want to be.

"It is connecting to those smaller steps that really anchors us to the people we want to be."

Don't get me wrong. The bigger goals are great, too—things like trying to get a full-fledged workout a few times a week. But if we solely focus on those things and dismiss the four-flight morning walk up, then we are glossing over the intricacies that shape our lives.

When we define more of who we want to be and what values we stand for, we feel pretty good about ourselves. In a study done on happiness, researchers found that people who are connected to and practice their values show greater well-being.[3] This is something well known and discussed in various modalities of therapy—such as acceptance and commitment therapy, developed by Steven Hayes.

When I get to my office floor in the morning after schlepping myself and the two different bags that I use throughout the day up the stairs, I feel out of breath, sure, but also like I just did something of value *for me*.

What is a health value of yours? What are the bigger goals—the "end goal"? The smaller goals? So often, identifying the end goal helps define more precisely the small, baby steps we need to take to get there.

Perhaps as important as setting the goal is setting the *intention* you will use to get there. Can you set an intention with how you will try to be with yourself when it comes to stretching your body's ability?

Often, my intention is self-kindness. I will push myself, but only so much, always honoring and paying attention to where I am at.

Give It 60 Percent

Several years ago, I took an eight-week mindfulness-based stress reduction (MBSR) course. It is an eight-week course developed by Jon Kabat-Zinn that teaches the basics of practicing mindfulness. When we began the yoga component of the group, the instructor said something that I loved, something I still tell myself when I am having an off day.

> **"Give it 60 percent."**
> **"Not 100 percent, but 60 percent."**

"Give it 60 percent."

Not 100 percent, but *60 percent.*

Some people may have a hard time with this. "Why shouldn't you give it 100? Isn't saying 'Give it 60 percent' taking the easy way out?"

I think the answer to this depends on your intention. You know you best. If you have a pattern of avoiding hard work, you may want to double-check that you aren't using the 60 percent rule to get out of challenging yourself. But for those of us who are used to pushing ourselves, we can find tremendous freedom in the 60 percent rule.

Do you know who I have found to have a hard time hearing the 60 percent rule? That's right: parents. When I suggest this to my teenage clients who are dealing with perfectionism—in front of their parents—a parent often comes back with something like, "Maybe we could aim for a higher number? Maybe 80 or 90 percent?" Well, we know where that perfectionism comes from.

My gut says that if you are reading this, you are probably not someone who likes to take the easy way out. You are probably a hard worker, maybe even a perfectionist. We are usually the kind of people drawn to self-help books.

One reason why anxiety and depression are on the rise, especially in younger people, might be the unrealistically high expectations they have set for themselves.[4] And we all know, at least on some level, that perfection is not possible. Or healthy. We are humans and are therefore fallible—and this is the way we were created. There is a benefit to fallibility. We learn from our mistakes. Self-esteem and resilience are built from falling and then getting back up. In a *Psychology Today* article, Dr. Grant Hilary Brenner describes perfectionism as the pairing of unrealistically high standards with harsh self—and other—criticism. Perfectionism is related to lower satisfaction and success in relationships, among a variety of other detriments.[5]

This trend of increasing perfection was highlighted in a recent 2018 study published in the *Harvard Business Review.*[6] The researchers found that from 1989 until 2016 college students' degrees of perfectionism, measured in several different ways, all increased significantly. This means that young people today have higher self-expectations, feel that other people have higher expectations of them, *and* have higher expectations of other people.

A striking find in this study was that of the different domains of perfection that were studied, the one with the most significant increase—an almost twofold increase—was that of *socially perceived demands.* That is, younger people today are twice as likely to feel high demand from people around them. This is linked to higher rates of developing depression and anxiety, among other mental health–related disorders.

This is something I see often in my clinical practice: young people who put so much pressure on themselves to succeed and exceed expectations on so many things they apply themselves to. Many times, this pressure isn't coming from their parents but is self-imposed. Many of their peers and friends have the same schema, and this burden they feel from their cohorts exacerbates their own sense of perceived demands. These young adults are so worried about failing in any area of their lives that they struggle with intense feelings of anxiety and depression.

Giving it 60 percent—in a world where we expect ourselves or are expected to give it 110 percent—is a tremendous act of self-compassion and generosity and may even lead to greater well-being and happiness.

I found this personally applicable when I was trying these yoga poses while pregnant. Having the leader give us permission to "give it 60 percent" was true kindness and helped me learn to be with my body in a way that felt nurturing and not harsh. Perhaps if the instructor hadn't offered this piece of compassion, I may have expected my pregnant body to show up to the yoga in the way nonpregnant me could have, which likely would have led me to throw in the towel and not attempt any of the yoga at all.

Learning to adopt this mindset helps us stay with difficult things.

"Pushing ourselves too hard for too long and setting unrealistically high expectations for ourselves can quickly lead to burnout."

That is, pushing ourselves too hard for too long and setting unrealistically high expectations for ourselves can quickly lead to burnout. Burnout is the feeling we get from holding sustained stress and pushing ourselves too hard for too long a period of time. If we don't pause and rest, or adjust the rigid and unsustainable rules we set for ourselves, there's a good chance we'll lose our desire to keep going, and we will certainly develop negative associations with what we are doing.

When I try to give my 100 percent across the board, it's just not realistic. Or self-compassionate (more on that later). I will get burned out. But if from the get-go, I set realistic expectations and reassure myself that I can tolerate a 60 percent outcome, I take off a big load of pressure and enjoy the process more.

See, the 60 percent rule is not really about doing it at 60 percent; it's reinforcing the message that we will be okay if that's all we get. In essence, it's detaching ourselves from the

> "The 60 percent rule is not really about doing it at 60 percent; it's reinforcing the message that we will be okay if that's all we get."

outcome and encouraging us to stay with the process and be pleasantly surprised if we do more than we set out to do. It's training ourselves to not focus on or put too much stock in the end result, because when we do this, our task turns heavy and draining, and we are likely to burn out, lose pleasure in what we are doing, or give up altogether because it just feels like too much.

The irony is when we learn to take some of the pressure off by allowing ourselves to do less, we actually do more, and for longer. We don't burn out as quickly and tend to come back to it, because the experience *wasn't dreadful*.

Answer these questions:

What are some notions and beliefs you have about your body? Are there things you don't even attempt to do because of what you think your body can or cannot do?

What is the narrative you are telling yourself about your
body and your physical capacity?
Are there physical exercises you do—with dread?
This may be an excellent opportunity to practice being with
your body in a different sort of way.

This is not to say that physical limitations are not real. They most definitely exist. This is about the mental limitations we put on ourselves without even realizing it.

Try putting this into practice:

Take a few moments and connect with your body—the one and only body you've got for your whole life. Please, please, do this exercise with care and love. As if you are coddling a tiny baby. Sometimes noticing your body—especially when there has been illness, pain, or trauma—can be quite triggering. Notice any judgments that come up in your mind as you do this exercise. See if you can notice those thoughts and then let them go. If any area of your body feels too sensitive, it is okay to skip over that area. If noticing your legs is too much, give yourself permission to focus on a less complicated part of your body. However you customize this exercise for yourself, see if you can come at it with kindness, compassion, and a recognition that you are complete.

Start from your toes—the ones you were born with and that
maybe were tickled as a baby. Move to your feet and legs—the
very ones that have carried you since you started walking. Just
think about that for a minute. Those legs—the ones you can look
down right now and see—they have carried you since birth.
Where have they carried you to? Down the aisle to get married,
to the hospital to have a baby, into scary interviews and classes,
and to sessions with your therapist. Let's have some gratitude
for those legs. And next time you are exercising, and cussing

under your breath, consumed with thoughts of how much you utterly hate the exercise you are doing, try noticing the sensations inside your legs and what they can do, all by themselves, without you even thinking about it.

What have they already done, and what more will they do?

What about your arms, your hands, your torso, your face? This one beautiful, miraculous, and precious body. How much gratitude do we feel when we connect with that?

9

Changing Our Relationship to Physical Pain

Open up your eyes; take in the landscape.

Migraines

Since I was twelve years old and in the sixth grade, I have suffered from migraines. The very first time I got one, it was in the middle of the school day, during recess. It was an indoor recess, and my friends and I were being rowdy in the classroom. I remember I was singing (I don't know what, or why) when all of a sudden I started seeing bright flashes all across my field of vision—very similar to the experience after a particularly bright flash from a camera goes off, and it takes a few minutes for the flash to disappear. Only these flashes didn't go away (not for a long time) and were followed up with a head-crushing headache and severe nausea.

When the flashes started, I didn't know what was happening and laughed with my friends about the "weird" thing that was happening to my vision. Looking back, I see now that it was one of those life-changing moments (as mentioned a few chapters back)—the sweet naivete of life before migraines and then the reality of living life with this condition. From then on, migraines were an ever-present force, lurking just beneath my current thought-stream as a worry and a *What if?* and a *When?*

Triggers for my migraines can be unpredictable. I have a laundry list of things that *might* cause them, but basically enough of anything can throw my homeostasis off. And so living with migraines means living with the unpredictability that at any moment, I could develop an intense headache with visual loss that feels debilitating. There is no rhythm to the frequency. I have gone for almost one year without them (hallelujah!) and then could have three in one week. It is really hard to know.

Living with this condition for nearly twenty-five years means that I have had my battles over the years—times when I have felt despair and self-pity, times when I have white-knuckled through my pain and made myself show up to my life even when I was physically suffering, times of intense anxiety and worry about the possible limitations attributed to my headaches, and, more recently, times of acceptance. I am not entirely there yet—perhaps a long way from it—but I can say proudly to both you and myself that I have grown in my journey.

And learning to dance with migraines has been a slow dance. The first decade-plus after their inception, I had a cowardly relationship with my migraines. I was young, I had a lot going on in my life, and I simply felt powerless against the enemy. I took them—and my experience of them—completely for granted. Their role in my life was predetermined—a foregone conclusion—an unfortunate, disabling condition that I would forever loathe.

The migraine would strike, and I would be overwhelmed by anger, sadness, and anxiety. I would stop what I was doing—leave school, work, or wherever I was, call my mother, tell her I had a migraine so that I would receive some compassion, go home, turn the lights out, and sleep. Every time a migraine would hit, my thoughts would spiral.

Oh, no! Why is this happening again? What did I do to bring this on?

I hate that I get these! Hate. It. Hate. Them.

I remember significant moments being crushed by a migraine: On July 4, my children were at the lake house doing sparklers. I was there, excited and happy, and did a little dance with one of them and, boom, a migraine. While I was getting ready with friends and family for the great solar eclipse of the summer of 2017 in Portland, Oregon, boom, another migraine hit.

I handed over the keys to my life to migraines and took a back seat. When the migraine was over, I would take back those keys, without ever making eye contact with the migraine monster, and get back in my seat. Hoping I would avoid attention from the monster by doing so. I rarely spoke about my migraines, either—talking about them was too anxiety provoking.

My relationship with migraines persisted this way until a number of years ago at my life-changing meditation retreat. We went outside in the beautiful nascent New York summer day, sunny and mild, to practice walking meditation.

It was my very first day of my very first retreat, and I was feeling both excited and silly.

And then it hit. The migraine monster came, loud and knocking at my door. In hindsight, now, I realize what a gift it was to have one while I was on that retreat.

I was in the middle of walking my path, surrounded by almost two hundred other retreat participants, when I started seeing those cursed light flashes.

Oh, no!

I moved into self-pity mode.

Great. I'm meditating and getting a migraine. Isn't that against the rules? Why is this happening to me? I can't stand these migraines; they are so disruptive and debilitating. I hate them.

All the while my anxiety was increasing and my breathing becoming more and more shallow. But then I chose a different path, so to speak.

The facilitator of the mindfulness retreat had said something earlier that resonated with me in that moment. While instructing how to do a walking meditation, he said, "Take in the landscape before you as your eyes sweep the horizon and you turn around on your path."

As I caught myself in the downward spiral of my thinking, these words came to my mind, and I thought, *Why don't I try taking in this landscape before me, flashing lights and all? After all, this is my landscape right now, and there is nothing I can do to change it.*

Though I had been seeing flashing lights for close to twenty-five years, it was the very first time I really looked at them and noticed the way they were affecting my vision and what I could or couldn't see. In the past, the anxiety I felt around them was so scary to me, I would have the experience of flashing lights cloud my vision, ironically without truly seeing or noticing them. And now, I opened up my awareness to notice all that my vision was offering me, flashing lights and all. It was empowering and kind and transforming.

It was an *Aha!* moment.

It was the first time I ever realized I could really take an honest look at those flashing

> "I opened up my awareness to notice all that my vision was offering me, flashing lights and all. It was empowering and kind and transforming."

lights. I could face the fear of what the flashes represented and not have the fear control me. Not that the fear would go away, necessarily, but now I had a way to notice my experience more fully and compassionately. I could start holding on to the keys of my car and look the migraine monster in the face. I could let it buckle up next to me in the passenger seat but not allow it to take my driver's seat.

Now, don't get me wrong. There is no magical ending to this story. My migraine didn't miraculously disappear because I chose to embrace what my eyes were seeing in that moment (and if you are living with migraines, I encourage you to seek advice from a medical professional to help manage them. I am sharing my experience here anecdotally, only. Please seek the advice of a medical professional about your pain). It also was not easy to do this—and continues to be a big work because I have such intense emotions embedded in my experience of them. But I did teach myself a powerful lesson about the degree of choice I have in living with migraines and how I could shift my relationship with them—expanding from the anxiety and anger that had been governing my experience of them for years into a more direct and honest look at my encounters with them.

I had spent so much time trying to figure out triggers to my migraines, trying to solve the mystery of what set them off so that I could avoid them. I had spent very little time paying attention to my response to the migraines once one had set in. I started thinking that perhaps my anxiety-and-dread response was *contributing* to the magnitude of the headache.

Furthermore, I started hypothesizing that by allowing myself to basically check out of my life when I got a migraine, I may have been unknowingly reinforcing them by dropping out of life—and all of my stressors and responsibilities—the moment they set in.

It wasn't ever meant to be, but having a headache was an "out" for me in life. I got to jump ship for the rest of the day. I didn't want to do that; I felt bad about having to do that, but still the thought remained: if I pushed myself to stay present with my life while I was enduring these headaches, would I diminish the reinforcing quality of being able to take a day off and perhaps, therefore, decrease the frequency of these migraines? These migraines are no joke, and those feelings of sorrow that come along with them are no joke either. But if I could change my relationship with them, I could take back control and start being the choice master of my life.

Now, I must admit, that initially, after I had this radical mindset shift of how differently I was going respond to my migraines, I may have taken it too far. At times, I became my own cruel soldier, and when I had a headache, even a particularly bad one, I would not lie down because of my reinforcement hypothesis. Some of this was pushing myself, striving, for a different outcome, and not truly listening and respecting what my body was telling me it needed. Because often, lying down in response to pain is important. Other times, I didn't need that, or was in a situation where I couldn't do that, and continuing with my schedule was just what I had to do. Please remember not to push past your own body's pain limits! Also, please remember that I am talking about my own experiences with migraines anecdotally, and you should follow your medical professionals' advice. What I want to impart here is far less about the *content* (i.e., having migraines), and more about the *process* (how we relate to our painful experiences).

Since then, I have found more of a balance through trial and error and careful listening. I am learning to tune into my current experience, and if I can and need to, I allow myself to take a break; if I am not able to continue with my day or don't need a break, I keep going.

How are you with experiencing physical pain in your body?

Pain is something we all experience in our own ways and to varying degrees. For some of us, this means living with a chronic illness or pain condition. For others, it is experiencing pain in more transient ways—things like stubbing your toe, or dealing with muscle soreness after a workout, or the aftermath of an accident. *Pain* is a big word and means different things to different people—even to the same person at different points of her life.

I would be remiss if I didn't follow up my previous discussion about connecting to your body in a more mindful and intentional way filled with self-love and compassion by talking about the pain we can experience in our own bodies. It is far easier to connect with our physical selves when we are feeling good and a more difficult task if there is an uncomfortable and intense sensation in our body. However, we can still practice kindness (and this becomes even more important!).

If you are fortunate enough to not experience much in the way of your own pain, do you know someone who does?

My guess would be that for most of you reading this, there is at least one person in your inner circle—close family and friends—who struggles with some sort of pain issue.

Living with chronic pain is serious. It is associated with increases in anxiety and depression, among many other risks to well-being.

Whatever your connection to physical pain is, I'd like you to stop for a minute and get in touch with how the pain experience is for you, even if pain for you is a more transient experience such as a passing headache or banging your elbow. The last time you experienced something painful—what was that like for you? How did you cope with it? Did you get stuck in your head and feel sorry for yourself, or angry—angry at the universe, God, a chair, whatever it was that you found to be the blame-worthy entity for the cause of your pain?

How many of you paused when the painful sensation began—when your brain began sending you messages that there was a hurt in your body—and stayed with your body? Stayed with the uncomfortable sensation of pain?

> **"We are so primed to respond to pain by checking out of our experience in one way or another that it takes real discipline and self-control and, yes, compassion to stay with the pain experience."**

We are so primed to respond to pain by checking out of our experience in one way or another that it takes real discipline and self-control and, yes, compassion to stay with the pain experience. (Again, if this is in line with your medical professionals' advice.)

"Checking out" could be getting lost in a stream of cursing.

It could be getting stuck in a thought avalanche of negativity and helplessness.

It could be anxiety about what the future holds for us, given whatever condition we are dealing with.

It could be numbing and distracting ourselves because we are too afraid of the pain to allow ourselves to feel it at all.

Some pain may be so intense that we choose to (or our doctors recommend that we) intentionally avoid the pain. Of course, follow your doctor's advice and your own wisdom in what you need to do to take care of your body. Approaching however you choose to respond to your pain *deliberately*, from a place of consciousness, allows us to be more mindful and aware.

It could also mean ignoring the pain, being a ruthless dictator and making ourselves forge on, no matter what is going on with our bodies, because we can't bear the thought of having to slow down or take a break and give to ourselves because of the pain.

What are you doing with your pain, both big and small? Is there anything you can do for yourself that will allow you to be more present for your body when it is in pain, and thus show yourself more self-compassion?

In a study done on the relationship between the experience of pain and the practice of mindfulness, researchers found that participants who completed two weeks of mindfulness practice reported significantly less pain-related stress in response to a painful activity than their counterparts who had engaged in a two-week relaxation program.[1]

One of the earlier studies done on the effects of practicing mindfulness on the experience of pain comes from research done by Jon Kabat-Zinn. He found that after participants with various chronic pain conditions engaged in a ten-week meditation program, there was a significant reduction in their pain indices, independent of the specific type of pain the individual exhibited.[2] These were all people who had chronic pain that had not improved with traditional medical care.

In a recent study done of sufferers of chronic pain who developed an opioid addiction, researchers found that participants who received methadone and engaged in a mindfulness training intervention were better at controlling their cravings and reported significantly more improvements in their stress, pain, and positive emotions than those who received methadone and standard counseling.[3]

Discipline and Kindness

I was raised in a high-discipline environment. We didn't talk much about self-kindness or learning to listen to ourselves. The key to thriving was to follow the rules as best as you could. So, many details of every day were accounted for and life was guided by *shoulds* and *shouldn'ts* and *allowed-tos* and *not-allowed-tos*.

Discipline was a large element of this way of life. We were taught that life's greatest fulfillment and meaning were held in these strict practices, and this would *lead* to happiness and joy.

The only problem was, I didn't feel happy. I didn't like many of the stringencies I was living with. If I had a question or conundrum—where to go to school or whether I needed to adhere to a religious commandment, for example— I asked a rabbi or mentor, and they advised me what to do. Oh, how I wish I was given guidance that included a deference to the self and to one's inner wisdom when deciding what was best and good for me. The best form of mentorship provides guidance and perspective but always with the implicit message that the individual ultimately knows what is best for them. This forms the basis for a healthy therapeutic relationship.

On the other end of the spectrum, some of us (myself included) run the risk of too much self-kindness where it borders on indulgence and narcissism or selfishness. These are the values of much of our Western culture today. *I want it, and I want it now.* Patience is no longer a virtue. Everything revolves around *me, me, me.* If we are not happy right now, then this is a very big problem.

This balance between self-kindness and discipline is an important one because we need both to live our best lives. Discipline is hugely important in achieving goals, being committed to those things that are truly important to us. Our lives

> "This balance between self-kindness and discipline is an important one because we need both to live our best lives."

depend on discipline. The *quality* of our lives depends on discipline. Healthy relationships require a boatload of discipline. We wouldn't get anything done without discipline. And actually, discipline, when practiced correctly, is a tremendous act of self-love.

However, discipline without self-kindness leads to *striving*, a cold way of being with ourselves, and ignoring the *soft animal of our body* (taken from Mary Oliver's "Wild Geese"). We can become harsh and unyielding. That's when we start to wash our faces a bit too roughly and catch ourselves in a constant self-critical thought loop. I think discipline without kindness is part of what leads to perfectionism, a rigid and unyielding way of living life, as we discussed earlier.

The balance of both can lead to a beautiful life—the disciplined pursuit and commitment to goals and a value-driven life balanced with a softness and gentleness with which we choose to pursue those important things. Discipline and self-kindness both are related to the *what* and the *how* of our pursuits, and we need them both to find balance.

How would you coach a friend if they were having pain? Would you judge them and pressure them to keep on moving? I don't think so. Most of us would encourage them to take care of themselves; we'd probably display empathy for them and what they are going through and tell them they need to take care of themselves. We might even offer to help take care of them, offering to watch their children or pick something up from the grocery store for them.

What is preventing you from being this way for *yourself?* (Asked in the gentlest of ways.)

Let's work together—collectively—and learn to turn that love and care inward. Let's begin to take better care of ourselves so that our children have a role model and see what it really looks like to be compassionate. How do you think these little people are going to learn to take care of themselves if they see you working yourself to the ground, or being a militant soldier to your pain? They need their parents to embody a balanced relationship to themselves.

We all know kids are little sponges—they pick up on everything and anything we are doing. It is very difficult to hide anything from your children. They pick up all the explicit and implicit messaging they are exposed to. They are paying attention, even when we think they are not. I still get a kick when my husband and I are having what we think is a quiet, private conversation with our kids in the next room. We will say an interesting word—say, "ice cream"—and all of a sudden, from the next room my son shouts, "Ice cream? We are having ice cream?" The same holds true for how we model experiencing pain to them. How do you respond when your child hurts themselves? You may want to refrain from minimizing their experience or having them check out of it. Saying things like "You're fine" or trying to distract them are training them to check out of their experience. Saying something like "Ouch, that looks like that hurts" not only is more validating and empathic but also shows them how to stay with an uncomfortable physical sensation (not that we should never distract—but not *always* distract. Distraction is but one tool in the toolbox.).

The irony is that when we embrace the totality of who we are—the strong pieces and the vulnerable ones—we get to a place of true wholeness and well-being.

Discipline with kindness: that is what so much of it boils down to. I think this provides some insight into the popular debate of whether it is possible to find balance in life. When we integrate discipline with kindness in how we go about living our lives, we are on the path toward finding balance.

> "When we integrate discipline with kindness in how we go about living our lives, we are on the path toward finding balance."

How can we find our own unique blend and balance for these two powerful operating forces?

If we err too far on the side of discipline, we live life that is disconnected from our souls and our bodies, a life that is harsh and rigid and oppressive.

If we err too far on the side of kindness, then we live a life of indulgence, aimlessly floating out of one day into another. We are not intimately connected to our goals or our personal development and shortcomings.

We need to find the equilibrium of the two.

When the two are in sync, we access well-being, contentment, and joy; we feel alive. We also notice the discomfort of challenge, of going beyond our comfort zone into an area of unfamiliarity or stretch, and in this space, we learn more of what we are capable of and incorporate those new feats into our self-concept until they are fused with who we are.

Expecting myself to climb those four flights of stairs early in the morning, even though the elevator is temptingly in my scope of vision? That takes discipline. Allowing myself to take the elevator because I am carrying a hot cup of coffee, or I slept really poorly the night before and am just too tired, or it is ninety-plus degrees outside and the stairwell is sweltering? Now, that is kindness.

Balancing these two forces takes honesty and awareness. We need to first learn to trust in ourselves to know what we need in a given moment to be able to determine if an act of kindness is just that—assuaging ourselves with self-compassion—or a cop out, a way out of doing something uncomfortable. Is your leg really hurting too much to take the stairs, or are you coming up with something so that you can avoid that challenge and take the easier, more comfortable route?

Only you, in your own wisdom, know.

Answer these questions:

What has your journey been with physical pain?
What conditions have you dealt with in your life that are the source of physical discomfort? What response have you noticed yourself having to the pain?
Is there any way you can make it kinder, gentler?

On the flip side, notice what is right with your body.
What is strong and healthy? We so often emphasize what is
not working in all facets of our lives, including health
and wellness. Let's open up the narrative to include what
is painful and difficult as well as what is right and
working.

Say this:

I am always complete just as I am.
I am always complete just as I am.
I am always complete just as I am.

Part 3

In an article written for the *Journal of Transpersonal Psychology*, William Braud[1] discusses the phenomena of "wonder-joy tears": the reactions we have all had when we are moved by something that feels profound, a "confrontation with the True, the Good, and the Beautiful—an indication of directly seeing with the eye of the heart, soul, and spirit." This experience often comes along with such feelings as joy, gratitude, compassion, and awe and reflects an experience of "profound gratitude."

Have you had those moments when you were moved to tears, without being able to put your finger on why? Maybe it was the time you inexplicably found yourself crying at your child's first-grade performance or once when you were looking up at the stars with a beloved on a cloudless night. Perhaps you found small tears gathering in your eyes as you glimpsed your children through the rearview mirror on your way to school as they chatted with one another?

Enabling ourselves to slow down and appreciate—deeply—that which is already there is a conduit to a gutsy life lived fully and can fill us with profound awe. In the following chapters, we will discuss the concepts of gratitude and joy and how to access those wordless moments that are ever-present in life if we only train ourselves to notice them.

Our capacities to live a life of gratitude and joy are not context specific or dependent on anything outside of ourselves. It is possible to dig into them right now, this very moment, and allow them to become a part of how you choose to view your life, forever.

10

Living a Gratitude– Infused Life

Every day is Disneyland!

Gratitude is sexy in today's culture. People are posting their daily gratitude lists on their blogs, Facebook, and Instagram, and it's a big part of many popular coaching programs and books.

And there's a reason why practicing gratitude has become so popular: it works. Science supports the positive impact of practicing gratitude on our well-being. In one study, after only one week of participants practicing daily gratitude, their well-being was significantly enhanced as compared to a placebo group and a group that practiced a pride-based intervention (these people were asked to recall things they did that they were proud of). The gratitude group's well-being even continued to increase after the intervention phase, and the practice heightened their ability to access positive memories.[2]

In another study, gratitude was shown to help with creating closure for unpleasant emotional memories. In the study, people were asked to recall an unpleasant memory and then assigned to one of three writing groups: writing about a neutral topic, the unpleasant event, or positive results of the memory that they could be grateful for. Participants in that last group showed more memory closure, less impact of unpleasant emotions, and less intrusiveness of the negative memory.[3]

And even more, in another study where participants were assigned to either a home-based mindfulness intervention group, a gratitude-practice group, or a control group, researchers found significant reductions in stress and depression and increases in happiness in the mindfulness- and gratitude-intervention groups. This study was done over a three-week period, and participants practiced four times per week.[4]

So, we can see how beneficial gratitude is for our well-being and our view of the world around us! Honing our gratitude craft can serve as a balance and a buffer, reminding us of all the good in this world every single day. However, as with all hot topics, the concern is sustainability. How do we get this practice to become a part of who we are, and not just a passing phase?

So many of these popular topics become key words—ways to enter a conversation and say something relevant, and maybe a little self-important if we're being honest. Other similar words that are often heard in conversation today are *authenticity* and *vulnerability*.

These *are* important concepts. So let's give them the respect they call for and truly understand what they mean. Let's understand how we can practice these worthy notions in our lives every single day to make them a part of who we are.

What we want is a gratitude-infused life, one where we don't limit ourselves to a single morning practice of gratitude but where we incorporate this concept into our

> "Let's have gratitude running through our veins and right on out into this world."

entire day, our global outlook. When we set our gaze on something—anything—we see it through grateful eyes. Let's have gratitude running through our veins and right on out into this world.

Experiencing the Universality of Being Alive

Connecting to other people on this planet in both direct and indirect ways nourishes a sense of gratitude. When we pause to realize that there are so many people in this world—alive in the same moment as us, each with their families, jobs, loved ones, celebrations, and losses—we remember that we are part of something much greater than ourselves and that we are not alone. It makes me feel both grateful to be a part of this planet and aware of how transient our time here is.

This experience of deep gratitude and joy hits me at odd times.

Recently, I was at the supermarket during a busy shopping time. Most of the lanes were open with people lined up waiting to check out. Usually I go through similar motions every time: unload my cart, maybe take out my phone, make small talk with the cashier, and go out to my car. If I am in a rush, there is an element of impatience (it's a good practice: practicing loving kindness to the person in front of you who has a huge cartload of groceries when you are in a rush!). I am most often in my little bubble, only noticing what is going on inside me and within my immediate circle. This trip, however, I looked outside of myself and scanned the room. I saw lots and lots of people doing exactly what I was doing: unloading their groceries, looking at their phones, talking with the cashier, and checking out. I looked at the row of cashiers, each with their unique style, look, and personality, and I observed them as they checked out the customers.

It was an interesting perspective shift. I went from my inner bubble to noticing my outer bubble, and the result was quite amazing. In this simple shift, I now felt connected to all the people who were in the grocery store with me. I felt connected and appreciative of not only my cashier, but all the cashiers in the store, working to ring up the customers, put smiles on their faces, and make small talk. All of us in that store had our own worlds we would return to when we were done, but for that moment, we were sharing time together wordlessly.

In that moment, I felt connected to the other people in the store. We were all on our unique missions, buying what we needed (and didn't need) from the grocery store, showing up for ourselves and the people in our lives in this important way.

I felt connected. I felt grateful to be alive and part of the planet and humankind.

Next time you are out somewhere, try this. Pause, look around at the other people who for that moment in time are sharing physical space with you, and notice the connection and love that comes with appreciating our shared humanity.

> "Notice the connection and love that comes with appreciating our shared humanity."

It only takes a brief moment to move from living in our heads about what is on our docket for the day into a different stream of consciousness—one that is an in-the-moment observation with a noticing of the other. It is really a profound thing, to feel that shift from the inward experience to the outward. It brings with it the awareness that making this sort of shift is possible *whenever* we are with other human beings.

Most meditation retreats end with a beautiful closing (albeit awkward!) ceremony. During one ceremony, I looked around at the large group of people in the room, all of whom had just had their own individual experiences on a seven-day meditation retreat. The leader asked us to look around the room and make eye contact with the people our gaze fell on. Then we were told to remember that we would all still be out there, in this vast world, after we parted ways and left this cocoon-like experience: out of sight was not out of mind. Even if we might never see these people again, they would still be out there in this world engaging in this spiritual practice. I was hit, maybe for the first time, with the power and beauty of all people. Connecting to a deeper spiritual and divine element of our shared humanity.

We are all beautiful humans doing beautiful things. That is how I feel when I look around at a coffee shop full of individuals having coffee dates with either people or their laptops or when I am in a grocery store or a waiting room. I often spend a moment feeling the beauty of being with these exquisite strangers, and I am sometimes even moved to those "wonder-joy tears."

Gratitude for the Seemingly Small Things

When was the last time you were grateful to go to the grocery store? I mean like you felt real, actual, soul-felt gratitude?

Though it may seem counterintuitive, the fact that we *need* to go to the grocery store is a blessing. For starters, it means we are alive. For many of us, it means we have people in our lives to feed. It means we have money to purchase household necessities—food, diapers, produce, and perhaps even extras such as nail polish, dog treats, and art supplies.

Wow. That's a heck of a lot to be grateful for.

Our bodies are physically well enough to go shopping and lug our groceries from the car to our dwellings. There is so very much to be grateful for in this one seemingly small mundane act.

We can take this even further and practice gratitude for all mundane acts that we do daily, even those pesky things that we approach with dread. Sure, doing the laundry or the dishes can be a pain—probably my number-one most detested chore, actually.

And yet there is much I have to be grateful for in doing these dishes: that I have food, a family, a kitchen.

Instead of saying "I have to . . ." in relation to some task—"I have to go grocery shopping," "I have to pick the kids up from school"—replace the "I have to . . ." with "I *get* to . . .": "I *get* to go grocery shopping." "I *get* to pick up the kids."

I encourage you to experiment with bringing a mindful awareness next time you are doing something mundane— pause and reflect on what gratitude you can find in this one act. Don't just let this be a cognitive experience, though. Feel it in your *soul.* Your body. Pause now for a moment and focus on something you are grateful for. How does it feel, and where in your body do you feel it? Can you feel it in your eyes, your chest, your heart? Notice it as fully as you can and let it fill you up. Do you experience any mind- or mood-shifts as you do this exercise?

Every Day Is Disneyland

Sometimes, on those early-morning commutes, I have this mind-blowing thought: *Every day is Disneyland.*

Most of us wake up on many mornings less than excited about our upcoming day. I know *I* am guilty of this sometimes. I wake up tired, think about the long day ahead, and definitely am *not* filled with a sense of excitement and gratitude for being given the opportunity of a new day.

On some nights, after a long and tiring day and maybe an even more exhausting bedtime routine with my kids, I fall into bed with them to put them to sleep—clean jammies on, brushed teeth—and we lie there together. I feel their soft hand on my arm, and I take an intentional moment to revel in immense gratitude, *in this moment, everything is perfect.*

It hits me that despite my exhaustion and the chaos of the moments before, we are alive; we are healthy. We have a roof over our heads and a lot of love in our hearts, and I feel teary-eyed for how much I have—and the fact that it is all really borrowed. With great love comes a great mourning at how ephemeral all that we have—and *who* we have— really is.

It is easy to lose that perspective when the waters are a little stormier. When my kids are yelling at me (or I am noticing my blood pressure rising in response to something they are doing), or I am in an argument with my spouse, or I had a tough day at work, or I am feeling lost about some parenting matter and I am crying tears of frustration, those words don't come as easily to me, but underneath it all, they are still there.

In these moments, too, everything is perfect.

We are all alive, we have each other (even if the more difficult aspects of the relationship are feeling more present), we are blessed to be on this beautiful planet—even more so, in a beautiful corner of this beautiful planet. I look at the trees, I look at the water, and I have the thought: *Wow, I am so blessed to be alive. Right now. In this chaos. I am grateful.*

It's easier to be grateful during calm, placid moments or when the going is easy. Just as it is easier for our bodies to be still and quiet when we are relaxed and resting (rather than in a complex yoga pose). I get it. I have been there. I *will* be there.

> "Let's bring the gratitude into our perspective when life feels harder."

Let's bring the gratitude into our perspective when life feels harder: at the end of a long workday, when you're trying to give the kids dinner, and one won't eat (a dinner that they loved last week at that!) and the other just spilled their entire plate on the floor. If we tap into gratitude in those moments, pausing and noticing the perfection and gift of that particular chaos, we will have a fuller and more well-rounded experience of gratitude.

Right now, as I write these words, I am sitting on the porch of a house on a beautiful lake. I hear the water lapping against the shore and the birds singing around me. I hear the rustling of the leaves. I feel the sun on my body.

I am relaxed and at peace. It is easy to feel grateful in these moments of calm.

Bringing in gratitude when life is rockier is more of a challenge, but it makes the experience fuller.

And this is not to say that it isn't okay to wish for things to be different. Sometimes we find ourselves dealing with very difficult situations that we wish just weren't so. That's okay. That's human, and of course, we don't wish difficulty on ourselves. But we can make space for both—wishing that things were different together with an appreciation and acknowledgment that this is what we've been handed. This balance is at the root of acceptance work.

I heard recently of a woman who responds to the question "How are you doing?" not by saying, "Fine" but by saying, "I couldn't be better." Let's try that. The next time you get that question or find yourself self-reflecting, say: "I couldn't be better."

Because isn't that the truth? In this moment, no matter how hard it is, it is my *only* reliable moment. Asking or wishing for a different moment is an

> **"Because *this* is the moment we've been given."**

illusion, an impossibility. Because *this* is the moment we've been given. This one moment here that I am gifted is really all I've got. Wishing or hoping for something different than what is reality, while totally understandable in those tough moments, is really a bit of a delusion. If we learn to be fully awake and *in* the moments we have, we are more fully alive, alert, and present for what this life is offering us. And finding some means of gratitude is an act of self-compassion in those harder moments. As I have said earlier, research indicates gratitude facilitates well-being and dealing with difficulties. For most of us, there is more right than wrong in any given moment. Let's really show up for it, get out of our heads, and *know* that it really *couldn't* be any better.

The Wisdom of the Trees

For a long time, I was taught that certain specific religious rituals would lead me to spirituality and divine closeness. And some of them did. Maybe, if I went back to some of them as an older woman, they would affect me in a different, more spiritual way. However, in my early twenties, many of those rituals no longer felt like conduits to spirituality.

I started to reexplore my relationship to spirituality. I knew inside my heart that I was a deeply spiritual person who longed to feel connected to a higher power. But what I was doing wasn't leading me to where I wanted to go. The answer for me didn't lie in disregarding all that I was brought up with and abandoning elements of my faith that had been present my whole life. I didn't want to leave my Jewish community and seek connection elsewhere. I didn't want to abandon thousands of years of a chain that I was a part of. It felt too important to me.

I did, however, want to feel spiritual and alive on my own terms. I wanted to define and take ownership of my connection with a higher power.

I wasn't looking for spirituality when I began meditating. As corny as it may sound, spirituality found me on my first meditation retreat. I was meditating outside in this big, open field. There was a big old oak tree, one of the only trees in the open field, and as I walked nearby, I noticed.

I noticed the tiny blades of the grass and the even smaller dewdrops that balanced themselves so perfectly on each tiny blade of grass. I saw the bugs in the grass, already busy with their morning work. I saw this giant old tree and found myself wondering what this tree had witnessed in all of its years, watching thousands of retreats come and go, year after year: healing dance retreats, trauma-recovery weekends, many different meditation retreats, bearing witness for the summer camp these very grounds used to house. What had this tree seen?

And in those moments, meditating near that tree, I felt deeply, deeply grateful to be a part of all living things. I knew there was a higher being, the universe, whatever you want to call it, that orchestrated these microcosmic perfections. And here I was, silently observing the beauty unfolding around me in my tiny little piece of the world.

I felt gratitude, allowing the raindrops to drop onto my skin and listening carefully to the soft whisper of the trees all around me, noticing that in this silent space, the urge to dash inside and out of the elements was less present.

Nature is an extremely powerful conduit to connection and a recognition of the vastness of this world. Paying attention to the nature all around us, even the man-made elements, is eye opening and a direct path to spirituality.

"Nature is an extremely powerful conduit to connection and a recognition of the vastness of this world."

Science shows we access greater well-being when we are outside in nature. Spending just twenty minutes outside—sitting or walking or anything—has been shown to lower stress hormones.[5]

When I am in my zone, meditating in nature, I feel both spiritual and poetic. I wrote these two poems, two years apart, while doing walking meditation underneath that big old oak tree.

Teacher

Come, Tree, breathe with me. Or rather, let's breathe together,
as the wind whispers past, massaging us both.
Oh, beautiful Tree,
I bask in your shade as you sit, tall and proud.
Your fullness is beginning to thin.
Loss, and grief, and sadness know you too.
I am humbled before you. For your gnarled trunk
is no match for my young hands.
Let's breathe, Tree, as I bask in your wisdom.

Old Friend

Hello, again, old friend.
Change has been kind to you.
Though we are both more weathered now.
You sit there, stoic in your silence.
Do you see me?
Feel me? Know me?
Are you too big and powerful and wise and old to notice me?
And then, I notice you.
How your canopy
Once full, now showing some gaps provides shade for me.
How your leaves rustling back and forth sustain me.
And not just me,
But all this life around us.
These people,
Silently walking back and forth breathing you in.
These bugs scuttling around your
Trunk.
Making homes in your roots.
These squirrels,
Playing and eating on your branches.

This moss,
that lives on much of your body.
Thank you, Tree.
For letting me learn from you, again.
For helping me to notice myself.
For sustaining me, season after season, year after year.

To this day, nature connects me to spirituality. When I carve some quiet time for myself in nature for a walk, or simply to sit outside, and I bring my attention to the world outside me, I get anchored in the spiritual layer of this world that is ever-present—even glaringly in our face at times—and yet so easy to miss and take for granted.

One day I was outside with the dog in the early morning, my mind busy with what I had coming up that day. I was mentally thinking about my morning lineup and the inevitable morning rush that was waiting me: *give kids breakfast, get them dressed, get myself dressed, finish up lunches, get myself to work on time.* I was noticing some impatience as I waited for our dog to decide where he was going to go potty.

Then I noticed a magical hummingbird flitting around in a young tree not that far away from me. It was truly incredible, how fast its wings were flapping. And then, it was gone. It was a special moment, made even more valuable by the knowledge that, had I been keyed out, I would have missed it entirely.

And how much of these literally awesome moments are swirling all around us that we are missing on a daily basis? We don't have to go far to find them. They can be as near and close as watching your small child's stomach gently rise and fall while they sleep.

Actually, research has found that feeling awe, or a sense of wonder, is shown to relieve stress related to uncertainty.

Researchers found that when people who were waiting for uncertain news over which they had no control watched an awe-inspiring movie of a sunset, they showed significantly less anxiety while they awaited the news versus other groups that watched other kinds of videos. Exposing ourselves to awe-inducing stimuli—often found in nature—can help us deal with anxiety and the stresses of uncertainty.[6]

Digging deeper, other research has found the stress reduction of nature and religion—which can both inspire awe—were only helpful when people took a more distanced approach to the awe-inspiring experience. These researchers found that when the experience is too immersive, it may have the opposite effect. To get the most benefit out of an awe-inducing experience, it is important to self-distance—meaning take on a third-person versus a first-person perspective, like watching something as an observer.[7]

When was the last time you let yourself just be quiet outside or in another space that makes you feel spiritual? Give it a try and see what it does for you. Notice the impulse to want the conditions of your spiritual experience to be "just right" (striving!). What happens if the conditions are not? What is that experience like? Can you embrace it and put out the welcome mat regardless?

Sometimes when I am outside, I observe the big trees that are around me and their leaves rustling in the wind. Sometimes they move more aggressively, and other times it is more of a silent dance. Yet, even on days without noticeable wind, the leaves move, responding to the gentle caress of the air around them, almost as if they are whispering to one another, and breathing right alongside me. And I know in those moments, that our existence goes much deeper than I will ever know.

Let us let nature be our teacher. There is much to learn from the watching, the noticing.

> "Let us let nature be our teacher. There is much to learn from the watching, the noticing."

It always amazes me when I practice walking meditation how much I notice in my surroundings that I otherwise would have missed: the different-colored rocks in the pavement, the bugs, the contrast of garbage with nature, the sound my shoe makes as it connects with the ground, the feeling of my body being supported by the earth.

It is all there, happening—we just rarely partake in the fullness of any given moment we have.

Oriah Mountain Dreamer, in her poem "The Invitation," asks, "What sustains you from the inside when all else falls away?"

This captures some of how I feel about the importance of being by ourselves, in nature. In nature, we can come back to the memory of who we are, without external and internal confusions. Without the trimmings and shiny wrappings of distracting materialism. We can anchor ourselves to this Earth with all that we really, truly are. When it is *just* me, my consciousness and all that I am taking with me to my deathbed, what am I left with, and what is that experience like? Is it pleasant, unpleasant, anxiety provoking, calming?

What am I left with if I let everything else fall away?

When you have some time on your own, try this as an experiment. Go outside. Observe. Notice what thoughts and feelings come up for you and observe those too. Choose some detail to pay attention to—a bug, a leaf, a flower, a drop of rain—and marvel. Just allow yourself to be in the middle of all things, with the knowledge that you are strong, solid, complete, and whole and a part of it all. You always were, and you always will be. You belong here, amid all other things. Once we get over the illusion of separateness from other people, animals, and things, we can find a peace, a healing, in knowing separateness is an illusion and that we are all a part of one another, and all belong to each other, right where we are. This awareness, my friends, brings immense gratitude.

There is beauty all around us if we would only open our eyes to it.

Finding Beauty in Surprising Places

I remember last January 1, 2020 (little did we know what was coming our way, eh?), my family and I went for a New Year's Day hike near the waterfalls in Oregon. It was one of those days where the weather kept on switching from sunny to sudden downpour in an unpredictable kind of way. We were hesitant about the hike but decided to go for it. As we got closer to our destination, the cloud cover thickened. It still hadn't started to rain when we go there, so we got out, hoping we'd make it back to the car dry enough after our short hike. Needless to say, shortly into our hike the heavens opened up, and I, my husband, our two children, and our very fluffy dog found ourselves getting drenched in a downpour. My first impulse was to draw everyone in, caution my children to avoid puddles, and make my body tense and small as I tried to escape the wetness. At some point, though, as I looked around at the rain and my kids enthusiastically stomping in puddles (even my dog didn't seem to mind too much), I surrendered. I laughed. We laughed. We ran back and were so grateful to get back to the dry of our car, all of us thoroughly drenched. It was a precious moment, a memory that will far outlast a pleasant, sunny-day hike.

I made a big move, East Coast to West Coast, a number of years ago. I now live in an eccentric region of the United States known as Portland, Oregon. Portland is known for its weird vibe—in fact, its adopted motto on billboards is proudly displayed: *Keep Portland Weird.*

In addition to its weird factor, Portland also has a reputation for significant rainfall and overcast skies. In fact, it averages thirty-eight inches of rain, only three inches of snow (compared to the national average of twenty-eight inches), and a whopping 144 days that the sun is shining per year. That means 221 days of the year have cloudy skies. That's a lot of cloud cover.

Needless to say, when we first moved from New York to Portland, this gloomy little fact was hard to digest—and even harder to embrace. Then something happened a couple of years in: I started seeing the beauty in the clouds and the rain. We live in a hilly area (many areas in Portland are very hilly), and on rainy days, low-lying clouds rest in the hills surrounding us. While they do not hold the energy of a shining sun, clouds do have something poetic, mystical, and beautiful about them. Sometimes, as I am driving home, a particular intersection where the clouds meet the tops of the northern hills is breathtaking. I pause and allow the gratitude of being able to see the beauty in the clouds— something I once thought of as "so gloomy"—wash over me.

There is profound gratitude just in being able to experience the feeling of gratitude. Sometimes, when life is feeling harder, this feeling of gratitude can be elusive. Noticing how

> "There is profound gratitude just in being able to experience the feeling of gratitude."

wonderful it feels when we *are* able to access it is in and of itself a practice of gratitude. We really don't have to go far or beyond ourselves to find gratitude, friends.

Another thing I have learned is how to stop running through the rain. We've all had those moments where we get stuck in the rain. When this happened and I got caught in the rain, I would mutter under my breath, rushing through the rain drops, silently chiding myself for not being better prepared.

Sound familiar?

In one memorable moment, I remember looking at the puddles, frustrated I couldn't get a closer parking spot, and I decided to shift my relationship to the rain. Perhaps it's because I live in Portland, or perhaps it's my mindfulness practice. But now I notice my impulse to rush through the rain, through those wet moments, and instead I try to slow down.

Slow down in the rain.

I experience the sensation of water hitting my skin, the smell and the sound of rain gently pattering on the pavement, and the solitude of being one of the only people outside and maybe the only one not caught in the rush of getting out of the rain. Obviously, this doesn't mean that if I am caught in a rainstorm or monsoon (Portland doesn't get those), I won't rush inside. Sometimes just for the sake of practicality I need to try to stay dry! But slowing down in the rain adds a playful energy into the mundane moments that would otherwise get lost in the space inside our heads, as does attending to the beauty that exists in the moments when, for many of us, it is so much easier to notice the more unpleasant side of things.

And what a powerful metaphor this is. Can we teach ourselves to slow down in the metaphorical "rain" of life? Can we pause and truly notice how we are doing in the rough moments? Pay attention to the different facets of what is unfolding within us and around us? Remind ourselves that we don't have to scrunch our eyes, ball our fists, and *just get through it?* Going through hardship with a gentle awareness, a noticing of what *it is like,* is a compassionate gift we can all extend to ourselves.

What is something mundane you can bring some grateful awareness to? Maybe a household chore or your exercise routine? Maybe it is picking up your kids from school and bringing extra attention to the looks on their faces when they first spot you. Precious, right? And we miss those moments all the time because we are too entrenched in our thoughts and in the next moments, or prior ones. If we choose to train ourselves to bring more (not all, because we are not becoming strivers) of our attention to everyday occurrences—things we do day in and day out—imagine all the extra moments of gratitude you would be tapping into.

And it's all for free. It's all there, happening to you, for you, anyway. We just need to slow down and give it the time of day.

11

Mindful Materialism

There is a place for all this stuff.

Mindful Materialism

My early relationship to "stuff" has its roots in the problematic issue of American consumerism that is literally overwhelming our nation. The house I grew up in was a nice, new five-bedroom house that was filled with stuff—yet very little of it was intentional. And why was that? Because much of it wasn't ever really wanted or needed but represented a "good bargain" or a hard-to-pass-up deal. As with so many others, the amount of stuff we had represented the inauthentic relationship to the material goods we owned. How many of you can relate to this story of being unintentional and mindless with material objects?

I read Marie Kondo's book *The Life-Changing Habit of Tidying Up* several years ago, before she became a household name and a Netflix series. I fell in love with the idea of surrounding myself with things that sparked joy within me. But more than that, it got me thinking about the power of intentionally bringing in goods into our life that are really desired, and not just because it's easy or convenient.

After reading Kondo's book, I decided to practice her method and see if it shifted anything for me. This led to a full-on closet detox where I piled heaps of clothing on the floor, some of which I had been schlepping around with me since I was a teenager (I have pictures to prove it!). It was time to say some hard goodbyes to the items I either didn't wear anymore or that didn't make me feel joyful. I love clothes and get attached to clothes I have bought (sound familiar anyone?), so going through this process was emotional. I did what Marie tells us to do: I held up every single item of clothing and paid attention to whether it sparked joy within me. A lot of the items didn't. I thanked them for serving their purpose in my life, and I ended up donating heaps of clothes. Some goodbyes were easy, and others were harder.

Donating the poufy, expensive black dress I wore to my engagement party was a hard one. But the reality was, I would never wear it again, and it just didn't make me feel joyful. So out it went.

After completing this daylong project, I felt the magic of living in a tidy, clutter-free space. I noticed a freeing of energy and brain space in addition to loads more space in my closets (yes—closets; I had accumulated so much over the years). What I absolutely love from Marie Kondo's work is the emphasis on making the choice to surround ourselves only with things that make us feel joyful. Imagine that—a life where you look around your personal world, your most intimate spaces, and see only things that fill you with a visceral feeling of happiness.

For me, the emphasis is not only on the word *joy*, though; it's also (and maybe more importantly) on the word *choice*. We get to choose what we share space with—physically and emotionally. This applies to the humans who are in our life as well, but for now let's focus on material objects.

> "We get to choose what we share space with—physically and emotionally. This applies to the humans that are in our life as well, but for now let's focus on material objects."

We can't avoid materialism, at least not completely. Unless we want to go meditate in a cave somewhere (which does sound like a neat idea, at least for a period of time), we are going to accumulate "stuff." It's built into our culture, and we are primed from the implicit and explicit messages we are constantly bombarded with to want the latest new thing, whether its clothes, electronics, toys for kids, or what have you. And for those of us with children, well, we know the amount of stuff we collect after kids is exponentially higher than before having them.

While materialism and consumerism are big parts of our lives, people hold different values when it comes to "things." Some people are good with very little, and some people find great joy and meaning in having surroundings and accumulating things that reflect who they are. The important thing is that we are intentional in what we bring in. I know I love clothes. I am deeply impacted by my surroundings. If it is messy or I have things around me that I don't like, I don't work as well, and my mind feels more cluttered. I choose to write in places that are decluttered, or outside, because that is where I notice myself being my most creative. When I am wearing a sharp suit to a job interview, I know I feel and act more confident.

But regardless of the value you place on things, having things is a part of life. Enter mindful materialism.

My preference to be intentional about the materialism I bring into my life likely stems in a large way from my childhood. Growing up in a family of five children, even though we had more than many, there were still messes, tension, and stress over finances. When we went shopping for clothes, we would go to the clearance rack and buy up the same clothing item in several colors because it was hard to turn down a bargain and money was tight. I grew up with a closet full of clothes, many of which either were not really the right size for me or were pieces I didn't really love. I had clothes in my closet still with the price tags on them, because they were never right for me. I didn't understand the impact our material possessions can have on our feelings of happiness and took for granted that I would have all this extra stuff sitting around, taking up figurative and physical space.

Reflecting on the good-bargain value (i.e., buying things because they were on a good sale versus if we really wanted them or needed them) as an adult, it's clearer to me that this bargain-buying value is often a product of a scarcity mindset. There was big appeal in something being cheap, even though in the long run buying unnecessary and unwanted cheap stuff only led to more waste.

The message I am trying to impart is twofold.

1. Let's declutter and develop less of an attachment to our stuff.
2. Let's lovingly and mindfully look over our environments and be deliberate about what materialism we

are inviting into our lives! Having stuff is a part of life and can be a source of value and meaning for some people. Being intentional in what we allow into our spaces is the key. And reminding ourselves that we absolutely can bring this intention into our life, even though this can be a novel concept to many, especially those who were raised with a scarcity mindset.

When I was younger, I remember looking longingly at other clothing items in the same store—things I could only dream of having because they were too expensive and hadn't yet made it to the back of the store and gotten stamped with a clearance tag. I would touch the fabrics and feel wishful for a moment, but it was never on my radar or conscience to think that I could actually have these things, the ones that resonated deeply for me.

As an adult, I see the great value in creating intentionally mindful surroundings that reflect our essence and help us in feeling grounded.

It doesn't matter where you get your stuff from; if it's been donated or free, more power to you! But what *is* important is how it makes you feel. When you look at it or wear it, are you happy and lighter? Or does it weigh you down? When you hold the fabric or wear the outfit, does it move you, stir something inside of you, even if it's a small stirring? You'll know it when you feel it. You might notice yourself holding yourself differently—with a straighter back, eyes ahead, or even a small smile on your face. When you look at the object, do you sense peace, contentment, and feel like it's easier to breathe? You can practice this wherever you are. Take a look around your environment and notice how your body is responding to it.

Today my philosophy on the material stuff I own is that I bring home fewer material items, but I am usually pretty excited about what I come home with because it represents my preferences and tastes (I am still honing this art). It makes me feel so grateful to walk into my living space, knowing that I have autonomy on how it is decorated and what I am looking at. It includes objects I have chosen with love, things that make me feel happy, grounded, and peaceful.

> "If it doesn't bring you contentment, or there is something about it that feels 'off' to you, don't bring it home."

Again, this has nothing to do with how much something costs or where it came from; it has to do with how it makes me feel. Because the idea of *wearing* contentment (or peace or groundedness—whatever word resonates with you!), *seeing* contentment, *cooking* with contentment, *sitting* on contentment is worth it to me. If it doesn't bring you contentment, or there is something about it that feels "off" to you, don't bring it home—even if it means you will have fewer material things. We get to be super intentional with our spaces. They really do deeply impact us.

I want to name a difficulty that comes up for me as we discuss mindful materialism and letting go of items to make space for things that are a truer reflection of your tastes and preferences: it is easier to follow this advice and get rid of stuff that was brought in in a mindless way if you are coming from a place of privilege and thus have the security that if you get rid of this sweater, you will be able to buy another one—one that fits you right *and* fills you with contentment and authenticity. I don't know what a younger me would have done with this method, since if I got rid of something, I wouldn't know when it would get replaced.

But ultimately this is not about how much money one has. It has to do with how we relate to our material items. It has to do with creating an environment where we feel peaceful, comfortable, and are grateful for what we have. Where we have a healthy relationship to "stuff"—inviting in what is good and necessary, and watching out for the trap of materialism reflecting an avoidance of dealing with something deeper and more emotional. Being deeply mindful about the materialism we invite home is another form of practicing gratitude.

When we truly love and cherish what we have, well, now we have a whole new wellspring for the practice of gratitude. We step into a grateful relationship with our stuff. Though inanimate, our objects, our home furnishings, clothing, purses, and accessories, have a profound role in our lives. Without any of it, we'd be naked, bare. When we choose to surround ourselves only with objects we have brought in intentionally, we attain direct access to a stream of joy, gratitude, and a specific intentionality with which we live our lives. When I put on an item of clothing I love, I feel confidence and authenticity and gratitude in being able to make this choice that without a doubt carries forth into my day.

When we wear things we truly love, that represent who we are and reflect our likes, and that fit us well, we carry ourselves differently. I know I feel more confident and "on my game" when I am wearing something I love. Right now I am wearing a cute and cozy black jumpsuit, even though I am home alone and writing. Wearing something I really like makes me feel sharper and more at ease than if I was wearing something I don't really like, even though no one is here to see me. Again, I'd like to stress that there is a lot of subjective value here.

How we dress our bodies has much deeper implications than simply appearances. It has to do with self-worth and value. So next time you are getting dressed, pause for a minute and put on something that makes you feel true to who you are, confident and empowered. Watch how being clothed this way affects your posture. You'll know when you're wearing something that feels *right*.

Growing up in a strictly observant family, there was minimal choice in what I was allowed to wear. We had stringent laws of modesty. There was a strong value in conforming. I remember going into clothing stores and gazing longingly at the modern styles the mannequin was wearing. I would walk through the sections of dresses, pants, and blouses I knew I could not wear because they were either too short, too tight, too revealing, too masculine (pants), or too distracting. I made my peace with it at the time, because I didn't think that any other reality was available to me. The times I snuck prom dresses or jeans with me into the dressing room were filled with shame, longing, and excitement.

Needless to say, I grew up dressing in a way that was not entirely representative of who I was. I did find a way to make it work and enjoyed shopping and dressing with the options afforded to me. I even developed a reputation in my circles as a fashionista and a good dresser! Since allowing myself to dress in a way that feels true to me, I feel so much lighter. I feel more confident and like I can accomplish some of the goals that I never thought possible.

Along with my evolving clothing stylistic preference, my relationship to what I bring into my physical space—a.k.a. home—has evolved tremendously over the years. The very first apartment my husband and I lived in consisted almost entirely of unattractive furniture. We bought/took stained, broken things from other people or, alternatively, would find things on the side of the road, bring them home, and repair or paint them. In that tiny first NYC apartment, our "curb alerts" (as we affectionately called them) consisted of some mirrors, a window AC unit, a large children's dresser (before we had kids!), and many other things that I can't recall (or buried down quite appropriately into the recesses of my memory).

I was less than fond of many of our earlier home furnishings. I would get an angry twinge every time I walked past a garishly gold mirror we acquired from someone's garbage and hung in our entryway.

Now, while it is certainly humorous for me to recount our curb alert days, I also know it didn't have to be that way. I didn't need to keep that mirror—the one I hated and that (thank God!) broke in our next move so I didn't have to see it anymore. I could have just not hung it up and not had a mirror. That simple. Or I could have found something at a Goodwill at a price that was affordable to us. But the point is, I didn't need to have that item in my house, let alone in a place I would see it multiple times a day. Does this resonate for any of you? Having something in your house you see all the time that you don't like and also don't really need?

Our next apartment was slightly better, with fewer curb alerts—we got rid of the stained dining chairs and replaced them with a dining set we bought on Craigslist. This one was clean and in great condition, but it was a style that was completely not mine.

Once in the Pacific Northwest, this idea of intentional furnishing and mindful materialism was certainly still evolving. We bought our couches used, for cheap—they were entirely too big and absolutely the wrong color, but they were comfortable. A garish red carpet completed the living-room look. But I was starting to develop this sense of surrounding myself with things we loved. At a garage sale, I found a couple of dressers I loved and still love to this day.

At this point, my home no longer has things in it I don't love (with the exception of a few compromises for hubby). And it feels wonderful. It is my happy space; I love being home.

What's your relationship to stuff? How did your family of origin relate to material things? How has this affected you today?

Is there any way for you to develop a truer and more authentic relationship to what you bring home and own? Are there some articles of clothing that make you feel more confident? Maybe try being okay with wearing more repeat outfits but only ones you truly love. Can you get rid of the clothes that no longer fit you? They only serve to take up space and make you feel bad about yourself.

Try practicing these same principles with your living space. What can you donate that doesn't make you feel happy or may even bring up negative feelings? It's hard to believe, but a lot of us have things in our homes that actually make us feel bad. But we don't acknowledge these feelings— we just take them for granted and move on. Get rid of the lamp or the rug. Be patient with yourself when bringing home furniture—remember, you may be sitting at that table or in that chair for years and years.

Think of your space as your sacred entity, it's where you get to be and hang out and feel calm and grounded. What kind of space would you need to achieve that feeling? How does it compare to what you currently have? How can you make the vision match the reality?

This is not to say we can't achieve inner peace and calm if our spaces are not just right. Again, we are not looking for all-or-nothing. It doesn't have to be—*shouldn't* be—perfect.

But realizing you have the *choice*, and making your space more authentic, is certainly a conduit to well-being and inner peace. It is achievable to attain a sense of calm wherever you may be,

"It doesn't have to be—shouldn't be—perfect. But realizing you have the *choice*, and making your space more authentic, is certainly a conduit to well-being and inner peace."

but it will be harder in a cluttered space where you are surrounded by things that zap your energy instead of filling you up.

A recent study found that people received some of the effects of coffee merely when they *saw* coffee beans. Imagine that. We are so influenced by our surroundings that our bodies respond to the simple (or not-so-simple) smell of the coffee beans. Another great study is one where the researchers found that people ate less and craved less when they saw greenery outside.[1]

Another study found that when a gift was *sloppily* wrapped, people tended to rate the gift as more favorable. Their conclusion? When a present is wrapped nicely, we set higher expectations of what we might find inside and are less happy with the actual gift. (This was true for friends, but they found that when the relationship was less close, wrapping it nicely did have added value.)[2]

In short, what we see in our environment affects our perception and behavior.

Let's just sit with that for a moment. Science shows that our surroundings impact our mood, even our physiology. That is pretty powerful. That's also probably why I often chose to sit in one of my favorite Portland coffee shops on many days when I was writing. It is a house converted into a coffee shop and has this cozy, friendly vibe that I love. It also helps me to look around at all the people in the shop, and wonder. What are their stories? What was their morning like? Who are their families? What are their triumphs and challenges? Sitting with our commonalities—the joys and sorrows that unite us all—fills me with joy, love, authenticity, and gratitude. Joy that in this moment, I have the privilege of being on this planet, with these people, and authenticity in the acknowledgment that we all carry with us a deep and powerful story that contains elements of joy and blessing. Though our stories certainly differ in detail, we are all the same in that we *have* a story that all hold very similar (if not the same) emotions—just in varying iterations—as one another. It's not about what we wear or what we have. It's about the way it makes us feel and what it brings out in us.

> "Our objects are facilitators in telling our unique story. Let what you wear, and what you surround yourself with in terms of material goods, reflect your authentic truth."

Our objects are facilitators in telling our unique story. Let what you wear, and what you surround yourself with in terms of material goods, reflect your authentic truth.

Before we end this chapter, I want to stress that while materialism is an unavoidable aspect of our lives, it is important to find balance with it and measure our attachment to it.

In our culture, it is far too easy to be sucked into an endless cycle of consumerism and things that can be truly distracting and take us away from true joy and meaning in life. We all know the cliché money can't buy happiness. And what a truth this is. More things might provide momentary excitement but will not lead us down the path of true happiness and contentment. That's why it's important to bring in a balanced, measured, and intentional approach to our stuff, learning to bring in only what we love and knowing that getting too attached to the things we own is a slippery slope. It's also worthwhile to explore your own attachment to stuff and consumerism. Has it become a coping mechanism for you? Is it a form of escapism? Often, if we find ourselves buying too much stuff or things we don't really want or need, it can point to deeper unresolved voids.

I picked up some beaded bracelets at a retreat I attended. I deliberately and lovingly chose the turquoise and amber beads because they symbolized independence, bravery, transformation, and truth to me. After I came home, I wore them every day. And then, one day, while I was on the treadmill at the gym, I took them off and forgot them in the treadmill cup holder. By the time I recognized my error, it was too late. They were gone. I looked everywhere for them. They weren't valuable, so I couldn't imagine why someone might have taken them. I was really sad because these bracelets had become something of a good luck charm to me. When I wore them, I believed myself to have access to more than what I was—more bravery, more wisdom. Not having them made me feel a bit lost and insecure.

And then I started reflecting on the surplus of power we sometimes give material objects and how an object really is just an object. While these bracelets held special memories, they weren't responsible for my bravery or insights. Those were all me, and I would still be just as brave doing scary things without wearing those things on my left hand. I made peace with not having them and, more importantly, gained awareness about how much emphasis I could potentially put on material things and decided I wanted to shift away from that. I owned my power, my bravery, and my resilience as things that were mine, not crediting them to a good luck charm. *Nothing* could add to that or take it away. I felt okay not having them.

Funnily enough, after several weeks, the bracelets showed up. But in their absence, I had found a deeper reliance on myself, and once I had them back, I no longer wore them as religiously (did you get the double entendre there?). And a few months after they resurfaced, they, unintentionally and quite symbolically, broke. The elastic that held the beads together got tired and gave way. There were beads everywhere, and there was no way I'd be able to collect them and restring them. So, I let them go. And because of my earlier work on material goods, I felt a sense of playfulness at watching the beads scatter and wasn't even that sad.

I'd like to encourage you to think about how you can bring a sense of intentionality and playfulness into your relationship with the things you own. Maybe choose a small but important space—your bedroom, your work office, or even your favorite bathroom in your house. Glance around it in a loving and playful way. Is there anything you can delete or move around or add to make the space feel more reflective of you and your tastes? Something tells me there will be. Give yourself permission to hit refresh and create some material change. And then notice how making a material shift mirrors a shift in your energy to something more exciting, fresh, and alive.

12

Finding Your People

Remember, you are not alone.

Some of us are lucky enough to fall into communities of like-minded people who support us and share some of our values. Places like religious institutions, kids' programs, or schools are perhaps easier, more natural ways to establish a community for yourself. Some people are fortunate enough to be given the natural circumstances for relationships to take hold and flourish.

For others, it is a harder task. For whatever reason it can be difficult finding your people. And to these people, I say persevere!

Don't give up! Because this thing—having a sense of

> "Don't give up! Because this thing— having a sense of community and belonging—is *that* important."

community and belonging—is *that* important. It helps us get through hard times; it allows us to share laughs and stories of the funny times. What we share, we bear. In fact, in a recent study, social networks were important in predicting health-related activity and overall health.[1]

There is something uniquely special about female friendships. Early psychological studies revealed the female wiring to connect with others, how we are primed to connect as a way of coping.

Women, in times of stress, tend to take care of their offspring—and get this—befriend other women. This response to stress is uniquely female and quite different from how men are wired to respond to stress. We females—both humans and many other mammals—form close, secure relationships with other females that increases in times of stress.[2]

Who are these people for you? Do you have even one friend (this can be a family member) who is someone who you feel supported by? Before you answer—know that a surprising number of people are feeling more and more disconnected. So please don't judge yourself if you're answer here is "no." You are not alone. That said, if the answer is yes—amazing! You have an established way of tapping into deep social connectivity in your life, someone who you can be brave and honest with.

If the answer is no—if this component is low or missing in your life, especially if you are a woman and especially in moments of stress—you may be feeling low or lost. Please don't despair though. Building close friendships is doable—and an active and intentional process. It usually doesn't come about by chance.

Take a moment to pause and reflect: what is the barrier in having these connections? Is it environmental—not having a strong community or reasons to go out and see people? Or is it something you are doing—isolating yourself, being too picky or judgmental, or having your walls up, making it difficult for you to connect with people—and quite possibility for people to connect with you? What can you shift in both your external and your internal world to connect more with others?

I had my own epiphany not too long ago. I was feeling let down by some of my friendships because I felt they lacked authenticity. I loved these friends but had a hard time connecting more deeply with them, which often led me to feel frustrated by our superficial conversations. I decided to try something new: I came forward with greater authenticity, opening up and speaking more about my own personal difficulties and truths. I watched my friends gently hold the raw information I shared with them and saw a shift in these friendships. They felt truer and deeper. My realization was that I was playing into, and responsible for in some degree, an inauthentic dynamic by not being more vulnerable with my friends—the very thing I was feeling frustrated with them for not doing! When I shifted the tide and disclosed more, they met me in this space and shared more as well, and the friendship embodied more connection and support.

Similarly, not too long ago I found myself at a community gathering, feeling somewhat the odd one out. I noticed circles of women talking and easily could have stayed to myself, with my narrative of not belonging or fitting in. Thankfully, I had the awareness at the time that I was starting to get pulled into a spin of thinking that would become a self-fulfilling prophesy, and cut it by walking over to a group of women and joining in the conversation. And you know what? It was rewarding on many different levels.

Maybe it is a mindset shift, moving away from worry thoughts and self-limiting beliefs. Maybe it is a recommitment to the value of friendship as being something innately important. Maybe it is a restructuring of your life, and intentionally putting yourself in places or situations where you are more likely to meet like-minded people.

In my younger years, environments like college made it easier to spend a lot of time with peers and build deep friendships. As I have gotten older and moved across the country (but even before then), I have needed to be much more intentional in developing strong friends. Coffee dates, going to events where I didn't know anyone else, taking classes that were of interest to me (hello, improv!)—all so that I was putting myself in environments where I would meet people.

Sometimes I was successful, and sometimes I wasn't. Sometimes I made friends, and sometimes I didn't. I have made friends only to have them move away, and that has been pretty devastating. But it's about grieving the loss, allowing those feelings to come and go and come again, and picking myself back up to begin the process anew. I have also been in situations where I've had to reevaluate if I was in the right community for me—if I needed to make changes so that I could have access to people who I had more in common with and it would be more natural to befriend.

Most often, cultivating strong social support doesn't just happen on its own. We have to be intentional, and so many of us feel isolated. I have heard this sentiment from both friends and patients. A feeling of loneliness is all around us. The reasons why is probably the contents of a whole different book. And we don't know how many others feel the same way. There have been times when I have shared lonely feelings with friends and been surprised by their shocked response—because I didn't come across as someone who was lonely. This may be you too, feeling lonely but appearing otherwise. And it's quite certain that there are people you know who look like they are doing just fine but are really feeling quite lonely.

So think about this, friends. On a scale of one to ten, how important of a value is friendship to you? And on the same scale, how manifest is it in your life? Look at these two numbers in a gentle and nonjudgmental way. The more discrepancy between these two numbers, the more of an indicator that you need to step up (compassionately and with ease and patience!) your intentional friend-making game.

Tiers of Humanity

We all need friendships, *deep* friendships, but we also need a more general sense of community. People with whom you don't necessarily share the intimacies of your life but who are in your life. The people with whom you talk about your weekend, TV shows, and likes and dislikes. Relating to these people is an important channel to feeling connected with humanity.

These are the people in my improv class or in the coffee shop, the ones I meditate with and smile at and never exchange a word with. Even the cashiers at my local Trader Joe's.

If we count our family as the first tier and close friends as the second tier, these general community members—the ones we see frequently yet whose names we may not know— are the third-tier people. They are important too. They keep us connected broadly to each other. Fourth tier are the people we will likely never meet in real life. Maybe it's your favorite morning news anchor or author. The people in our social sphere who we don't know in person. These people also provide us with an important sense of connection.

One subset of incredibly important connections in our life is that of role models. These are the people who inspire us, remind us that our dreams can become realities, and keep us anchored to elements in our life that are truly important to us. There are so many different types of role models, and they appear in our first-, second-, third- and fourth-world tiers. We can have roles models in many facets of our lives—in our parenting, careers, marriages, and so on.

In a recent study, researchers found that people were more likely to achieve their goals if they shared them with someone they perceived to have higher status than themselves—that is, people they perceived to have more prestige and respect. Working adults who shared career goals with someone they thought had higher status were more committed to their goals. College students who told their grade goal to someone they thought had higher status were more committed and more likely to achieve their target grade.[3]

In short, finding a role model, someone you look up to and admire, and telling them about what you want to accomplish may actually help you achieve your goal.

Social Comparisons (Again)

Whenever we are talking about relating to others, it is normal and natural for the human mind to go into "comparison mode." As we talk about the people in our lives, we could notice the mind's impulse toward comparisons and then learn to let those thoughts go.

Inevitably, the topic of comparisons comes up in much of the therapy work I do. It is human to compare and rate how we are doing relative to others we know (or think we know or don't know). However, comparison is a common thinking trap, and acts as a barrier to feeling happy and content, and ironically, to achieving our goals. I have said the words "you don't know what is going on behind closed doors" countless times in therapy. And I have been told that in my own therapy work as well. And how true it is! We may think we know, but we really, really don't know what is happening quietly for others. Even those we think we know well.

I think it's important to clarify here—when I say "role model," I don't mean someone to compare yourself to or to feel badly about yourself and where you are in your life. Be careful of that. I am referring to selecting people you admire who are a couple steps ahead of you and doing things you want

> "We *never* see someone's full reality. So, in essence, we are really comparing apples to elephants. Your life is just not comparable to anyone else's."

to be doing. These can be people on social media or people in your own life. Having a blend of people you know in person and people you follow is a nice balance. And if you notice yourself going into comparison mode, simply note it, congratulate yourself for noticing it, and then either let it go or challenge it with more accurate thinking. Then recenter right on back into your own life. Remind yourself that by their nature, comparisons are distorted and irrational thoughts. We are all placed in our own life with our own set of particular circumstances and contexts, and we *never* see someone's full reality. So, in essence, we are really comparing apples to elephants. Your life is just not comparable to anyone else's.

Comparisons are tricky and bring along with them much suffering. We don't need to compare ourselves to anyone else. It is irrelevant what is happening in someone else's life, and what they have or what we think they are doing better than we are. It's all a matter of perception, anyways.

The simple fact is this: their life is not our life.

Those comparisons rest on one big untruth: that how and what happens to other people is somehow relevant to us. It is not. We are all, each of us, on our own unique journeys in this life. Someone might seem like they are excelling at something that we are not excelling at or have something we don't, but the relevance is an illusion, because I guarantee you, my friend, that you have things they are wishing for.

"It's our ego that cares about what other people think, not our truest and highest form of consciousness."

And really, underneath it all, is the knowledge of this truth: an authentic sense of our worth and value will always come from an internal acknowledgment and awareness that we are good, *not* from anything outside of us. Sure, our pursuits and achievements feel nice. To some degree, it may be satisfying that we look like we've got it "all together." But really, that's an illusion too. It's our ego that cares about what other people think, not our truest and highest form of consciousness. If we can notice where this drive is coming from, and set our egos aside, we can learn to let it go by affirming that who we are is completely separate from someone else's reality, and who we are is enough. We can then really shift our relationship away from that pesky comparison thinking and back into focusing on our life and our next steps.

Practicing tools of mindfulness can anchor us to this truth. If you catch your thoughts going off on some comparison, notice the mind wandering in this direction and then bring your attention to an element of your present experience: your body, your breathing, your awareness of sound, your compassion, whatever you choose to notice in this present moment. Notice if the thoughts you are having might be coming from your ego and remind yourself that you can let those thoughts go. They are taking you farther away from yourself, not closer.

In Jewish tradition, there is a concept that we are all created "B'Tzelem Elokim"—in God's image. I think of this at times to help me get over my ego when it comes to other people. I look at them and remind myself that we are all holy, beautiful beings, and it helps me drop below my ego. Try looking at someone, maybe even in their eyes, and remind yourself of this when you find yourself comparing. We all carry a piece of Godliness inside of us—that is how we are connected and related to one another, in some way. The external trappings—our bodies, our stuff, our accomplishments—simply aren't how we find connection and relatability with one another. In short, the specifics of someone else's life have nothing to do with you. Let's focus on what we have in common and stop perseverating on the stuff that we don't.

In a fascinating study, researchers followed more than eight hundred fifth graders through their thirties. Participants responded to several surveys over the years that assessed things like physical health, mental health, and information on socioeconomic status. Those students whose parents and teachers participated in courses that focused on building stronger relationships with their students had significantly better outcomes in health and socioeconomic status. This science confirms our intuitive sense of the importance of bonds and relationships.[4]

Yes, we benefit from relationships. They are core to our mental health and well-being, and—read this slowly—they don't add or detract from your inherent worth. That's where comparisons get so tricky. We think falsely that because someone has done more in terms of outward achievement than us that they hold more worth or status. They don't. B'Tzelem Elokim.

As much as finding role models is important, it's the cherry on top to developing inner self-worth. That comes from within. While role models such as your therapist can help you find and affirm your self-worth, your association to them doesn't create it. There is a healthy place for role models and for connecting to people and activities that keep you anchored to your goals, but this only goes so far or not far enough if we haven't accessed our self-worth and these relationships become yet more fodder for self-doubt and comparisons.

So yes, acquire some role models. This can be one helpful component in keeping you anchored to your goals, inspired, accountable, and on track. Connect to other forms of your source of inspiration and meaning as well. Listen to podcasts, read blogs, or subscribe to magazines that are of a topic that holds value to you. But most important of all, know that these connections do not bring you any added worth. They are strategies. You don't need anything or anyone to increase your value—because that, my friend, is already nested well within you.

13

The Trifecta of Centering

The spirit with which you want to live your life.

Managing Stress

I began writing this book in March 2019. At that time, I started jotting down notes of what would be in this book and made the commitment to write it. Over the year, it evolved and took shape right up until, you guessed it, March 2020. When the world went topsy-turvy because of COVID, my book was just about done. As I've done all of my revisions in the middle of a global pandemic, I'm struck by how much universalness there is to the lessons in these chapters, and how going through a pandemic has exacerbated both the suffering that exists in this world and the need for grounding and self-compassion to meet it. One thing that has taken on new meaning since March 2020 is stress.

We have all been living with chronic stress for some time now. No longer reserved mostly for *some* people, *certain* ages, and *briefer* episodes, stress has become inescapable and ever-present no matter your age or location. Adults and children have all been greatly impacted by the stress of living through something so devastating. I have seen the effects of living with chronic stress personally and professionally. As humans, we are not well-built to sustain chronic stress. It takes a tremendous toll on our mental and physical health. Never before (at least in our lifetimes) has our world been so *stressed out.*

True, there are a lot of factors that we can't control in living with chronic stress, *and* there are always things that we can find that we *can* control when we are experiencing ongoing stress. Learning about stress, acknowledging it, understanding how to embrace and live with uncertainty, and figuring out how to cope with it are all places where we can find much personal power and agency in our coping with stress.

We throw the word *stress* around all the time.

I'm so stressed, we tell people when we are feeling overwhelmed in life.

Why are you so stressed?, we ask our partners when they are grumpy or snappy.

But what is stress, and where does it come from?

From my experience, both personal and professional, "stress" is the tense and overwhelmed feeling that comes from an overestimation of risk and an underestimation of our ability to cope with the stressor. It can also come from being in a demanding and overwhelming situation. It usually originates in response to some situation: from being late to an appointment, your child throwing a tantrum, having a hard day at work. It is anything that over-whelms us and affects our thoughts, feelings, and physical sensations.

Stress is a part of life. We can't get away from it—nor should we want to. Stress acts as a motivator too. It helps us prepare for a work meeting, research the right daycare for our child, and meal plan for our families. It is what can light the fire under our bottoms (so to speak) to get things done.

> **"Stress is a part of life. We can't get away from it—nor should we want to."**

So what's the problem with stress?

When it gets to be too overwhelming or too frequent, when we bump into problems that stem from our chronic stress, or when the feelings, thoughts, and body sensations persist beyond a reasonable time, we cross over into the category of anxiety. Clinical anxiety mimics the stress response to some extent, but it is a feeling that persists, feels unsolvable, is intense, and impairs our functionality. Whereas stress is often the response to a specific situation and resolves when the situation goes away, clinical anxiety is a pervasive feeling of dread that is not necessarily related to a specific situation or persists long after a situation has gone away.

What's *your* experience with stress and anxiety? Where do you fall on the continuum?

Write down these two questions or keep them in your mind as you read on. This chapter is about identifying some anchors that will ground you when stressful, overwhelming moments wash over you—as they inevitably do.

There are so many different ways to manage stress, and different things work for different people. I'd like to present what I call the "trifecta of centering": exercise, meditation, and personal connections. These three centering practices not only work for me personally but are evidence-based as well. I know that if I hit three out of three on the list, I have a day where I feel more grounded, am more efficient, and am ultimately less stressed.

Exercise

We all know how important exercise is for our physical and mental health. In fact, exercise not only has been proven to make our bodies healthier and increase our well-being but is also linked to increasing our ability to learn. Some research asserts that we don't need sustained, daily exercise to see these positive results, either. We can see brain-functioning sharpen when we exercise in short bursts, like a once-a-week game of basketball.[1] Not only that, but we are shown to live longer if we move more. This life-lengthening movement can be as small as taking the stairs instead of the elevator (as I have resolve to do), biking to work, walking more, and not necessarily putting up with a workout you hate.[2]

How are you moving your body?

If this is something you struggle with, see if you can start small. Commit to one shorter workout a week and move up from there (again, always check with your physician if you have any health concerns). Maybe put on some upbeat, pump-you-up music, which has been shown to increase how much you enjoy your workout.[3] Habits are created out of these small commitments that we can actually do and then building on them.

Notice how you feel after you've exercised. My guess is it will be pretty good. File that feeling away for the next time and bring it to the forefront to get yourself to move your body. I know I feel calmer and happier—not only right after I exercise, but for the rest of my day. Remembering how good we feel—or the intrinsic motivation we have in doing something—is a great form of motivation.[4]

Try it.

Meditate

As with exercise, it may be best to start small with meditation. Maybe this means five minutes a day while you listen to a guided meditation app. More and more research supports the far-reaching benefits of meditation, and it has been shown to improve mental well-being as well as physical health. A recent study even linked meditating to longevity![5]

Meditation is shown to help with anxiety, depression, stress management, attentional abilities, and cognitive decline. In fact, in one study, older participants who went on an intensive meditation retreat showed attentional gains seven years post retreat. The people who had a daily meditation practice benefited the most.[6]

On top of that, meditating has been shown to increase physical movement, so doing this one may help you exercise more.[7] Two birds, one stone, baby!

I personally find great gain and benefit from the more formal mindfulness practices, but not everyone does. If this doesn't do it for you (after you have given it a fair shot, enough to be able to say you've tried it in various mood states and spent prolonged time with it), then find your thing to infuse in your life to increase well-being.

We all find well-being in different ways. Spending time outside and marveling at nature can be one important conduit to well-being. But maybe for you it is physical movement. Maybe it's a blend of sitting and moving. Now might be a good time to reflect on what gives you a sense of well-being in your life.

Practicing acts of kindness is also related to well-being. I remember early on in the pandemic, I came home one day to find a chocolate bar with a note in my mailbox. The note was a compassionate offering of how hard it must be to parent during the pandemic and how "mommy Katz" deserved some chocolate and acknowledgment for all that she must be going through. The note was not signed. After going through a quick embarrassed yet humorous wondering of which neighbor might have seen me in a stressed-out moment, I landed with how finding this small-big token in my mailbox was a hugely pleasant surprise and made me feel so seen. I still have not figured out my mystery chocolate sender's identity (I asked my neighbors—it wasn't them!), but I think to myself, now *that's* a person who has figured out how to cope with big stress well. Maybe this is a great avenue for improved well-being for you to explore as well.

At another point during the pandemic, I was standing in a very long and slow-moving line to get into a supermarket. There was an elderly couple right in front of me in the line, one of them holding a cane. One woman from the very front of the line must have noticed this couple just as it was her turn to enter the store and came to get them to switch places with them. It wasn't pleasant outside, it was a very slow line, and this woman did what she felt was the right thing to do in that moment. I felt a joy at seeing such a deep display of humanity and compassion (these acts of kindness really stick with me), and I thought to myself, "Now, this woman is doing it right."

Social Connections

Connecting with others on a daily basis is linked to physical and mental well-being, and may even stave off dementia.[8]

Being socially connected runs the gamut of getting coffee with a good friend, seeing your colleagues at work, having a small chat with the cashier at the grocery store, complimenting someone on their shoes, smiling at another driver on the road, and so on. Each of these interactions counts and makes us feel good. Next time you have contact with someone, anyone, notice how it makes you feel. Bring this awareness to the next several encounters you have and use this realization of enhanced well-being as a source of motivation to keep on connecting with others.

I recently had the opportunity to say hello to someone, and I didn't. There was a new face at the gym, a woman about my age who I had a good feeling about; she just looked like the kind of person I would be friends with. We gave each other a smile, even walked past each other, but didn't talk at all. Just smiling at another human is a form of social contact, but I know that if I had gone out of my comfort zone and maybe said hi, I would have felt great about it, not because of the outcome—I don't know how that would have turned out, of course—but because I would have connected to another human, I would have stepped out of my comfort zone and tried something new.

These are all good things. I didn't do it today, but I hope to do it next time. The next time you are on the fence about engaging with someone in pleasant social contact, learn from my experience and go for it!

Exercise, meditation, and social connections are three things that keep me happy and grounded. What does it do for you? Once you've identified your three or four grounding practices, anchor yourself to those things every day, in small ways, to feel at peace and deal with the stresses of life.

Sleep

Okay, okay, I know I said *trifecta*, and I do think the three aforementioned practices are core; however, two more elements are basic in managing stress: sleep and self-care.

I know the challenges of getting an adequate (I won't even say "good") night's sleep. As a busy working mother, I know the challenge is real. There is so much to do in any one given day, and we are so often in the "doing" mode—putting on our work hats, then coming home and immediately trading them in for our mommy hats, and then, at last, when the kids are all asleep at night, we're lucky if there's still some evening time to put on our relaxation or partner hats.

Those precious nighttime hours, after all the little people are snuggled and asleep in their beds, are scrumptious. It is tempting to stay up late, get work done, or relax and watch Netflix. How many of us have found ourselves up really late—*too* late—watching yet another episode on Netflix? (And they all said "Amen.") We told ourselves we'd just watch one episode, and here we are on our third. We know we'll feel groggy and grumpy when 6:00 a.m. rolls around, but it is just so dang hard to have the fortitude to turn it off. The struggle is real, my friends.

I know, we have to do what we have to do, and sometimes, it does have to keep us up late at night, but I'm encouraging you to please, please, try as you may, *protect your sleep*. This harkens to an earlier discussion we had in chapter 4 on discipline and kindness. Practice discipline to plan out your days a little more intentionally so that you don't have to pull late-nighters (at least not most of the time); practice discipline to turn off the TV and kindness in getting your body to bed.

And for many of us, the journey is just beginning when our heads hit the pillow. For many, nighttime wakeups from the "wee beasties" (what Jamie calls the children in *Outlander*) are an every-night—or almost-every-night—occurrence. In one of my favorite comedy routines by Michael McIntyre, he describes that before having kids, he and his wife would kiss each other and say good night and dreamily fall asleep. These days, they wish each other "good luck" before rolling over and hoping for the best.

Sound familiar, anyone?

Therefore, making sure you are getting yourself into bed and turning the lights out is so very important, because we aren't even guaranteed how much slumber the night will hold for us from that point on.

And sleep is so, *so* important for basically everything. Science has shown over and over how important sleep is for our physical and mental well-being. Poor sleep or not enough sleep is linked to higher rates of depression, GI issues, and cardiovascular risks, among many other things.[9] Even not maintaining a regular bedtime and wakeup schedule and getting varied amounts of sleep every night may put someone at risk for a whole variety of metabolic disorders such as obesity, hypertension, high blood sugar, and high cholesterol.[10] Shorter-term consequences related to not enough sleep can lead to daytime sleepiness, irritability, trouble focusing, less work productivity, and diminished creativity and decision-making.[11]

I definitely notice I have a much harder time writing and being creative and am just grumpier when I didn't get a decent night's sleep.

So do yourselves a favor. Put a limit—even set a timer, if that helps—on your nighttime activities and protect your bedtime. Get an old-fashioned alarm clock and charge your phone away from your bed. Find ways to unwind before bed so you are more able to fall into a restful slumber, and find other times to do the important work you are doing late at night.

Self-Care

Ahhh, "self-care." Another popular word in self-help books and mom's groups.

Practicing self-care as part of your routine can help prevent burnout. It is good for your energy levels and helps with life satisfaction.

But what do we really mean by self-care?

Self-care means different things to different people. We have all heard of the outward self-care modalities: taking care of your body, taking time for yourself, even pampering yourself from time to time.

> "I would like to propose an expanded meaning of self-care: taking care of yourself by making sure you are connected to the spirit with which you'd like to live your life."

I would like to propose an expanded meaning of self-care: taking care of yourself by making sure you are connected to the spirit with which you'd like to live your life.

If kindness is a value to you, then this means taking the time to smile at the elderly person in front of you in line at the grocery store. (Yes, I go to the grocery store often, #momlife.) If presence is important to you, then it's making sure every single day includes moments of just *being*—by yourself and with others. Self-care is about connecting to your meaning in life every single day. It isn't only about the obvious acts of nourishment. It is also those more value-driven choices we make that can be quite hard to do and aren't immediately enjoyable. Of course, everything we've talked about in this chapter—meditating, exercising, socializing, and sleep—are forms of intentional self-care. In these ways, we care for ourselves by creating a beautiful cocoon-like existence for ourselves, where we are cushioned by the things that sustain us.

So take care of yourself. Nurture yourself. Attend to and practice the things that are so very important to you—the ones that make you feel grounded, connected, and purposeful.

This, too, is a form of self-care.

14

Finding and Redefining Spirituality

Spirituality lives within us and all around us.

I used to think that being spiritual was being religious.

I thought that the more *religiously observant* I was, the more *spiritual* I was. I defined myself as a deeply spiritual person, and on some level, I was. I've always believed in a higher power, that the purpose of life runs far deeper than what I can comprehend. However, I emphasized stringent religious observance over my own personal connection to myself and this vast world around us.

Over the years, I have moved my spiritual focus away from the religious stringencies (although some religious practices are still very real for me) and placed more emphasis on the *soul* of things.

That means recognizing at once how very small we are and that we contain immeasurable capacity. We are so tiny in this world, each of us just a little body of molecules traveling through the time we are given on this planet.

Before I found meditation, I used to think we were all like little worker ants—rushing about on their important missions, not knowing when their little lives would be snuffed or squashed out. This seemed analogous to the experience of being human. All of us, thinking we were on these big important missions, not knowing when our lives would be extinguished by some higher, distant, and not always compassionate power.

However, now I realize our experience of being human is so much more profound than that of an ant. Our brains are evolved; we are capable of higher thinking and therefore tapping into *meaning* in our lives. *Purpose.* Ants go on about their business, seemingly robotic in their motions. They are beings put into motion by some force completing their jobs in the time they are allocated.

> "We can tap into any and every moment we choose and find deep meaning and purpose."

This is not our human experience. We are capable of deep thought, perspective, and connection. We have thoughts *about* our thoughts—a process that is uniquely human. We think about death, another thing that is distinctively human. We can tap into any and every moment we choose and find deep meaning and purpose. We can connect with other people, animals, and this planet to create change and impact. This awareness is a piece of spirituality.

I feel my most spiritual when I am in nature. It gives me perspective on just how old this Earth is, and how young

I am—really, we *all* are, even my grandmother who lived to her nineties—and how privileged I am to be given this opportunity to traverse through some time here, or have time traverse over me. It helps me realize how fleeting life is and turn this into gratitude for the time that I have. It *still* helps light a fire in me to be brave and tap into my personal longings and purpose. It makes me realize that life goes far beyond *human* life—there is life all around us, in the whisper of the wind, the rustle of the trees and the grass, the song of the bird.

There is wisdom to be found in nature, too. Everything works *just so* to create and sustain this beautiful world—it's miraculous. Everything knows what to do, and a beautiful symbiosis exists between us humans and all other living things. We need each other to survive. We cannot exist independently; people need other people, and all other living things as well. We can find our humanness reflected in nature as well—in the changing of the seasons, life, and death.

As I was editing this chapter, I was on a flight. The pilot made his standard announcement at the beginning of the flight, telling us the time of expected arrival and the expected weather conditions. He said with confidence that the weather was calm and it should be "smooth sailing."

Toward the end of the flight, he came back on over the loudspeaker and said, "Flight attendants, take your jump seats, please; we're going through some turbulence."

The words *jump seats* immediately got my attention.

And then we went through the heaviest turbulence I think I've ever experienced. I was sitting roughly in the middle of the airplane, just watching the plane in front of me tilt up and down. The man on my left grabbed his wife's arm. The man on my right was throwing up. And then the turbulence was over.

I found myself thinking about just how vulnerable we are in a little airplane in the vast sky, at the whim of Mother Nature.

But really, we are *always* that vulnerable.

My current spiritual journey is all about finding a balance between religious observance—parts of which still hold significant value for me—and opening up my eyes to the deep spiritual wellspring of the world around us. Having some sort of spiritual connection gives life meaning, helps us live with pain and suffering. Finding spirituality can enhance our life in this world. There are even studies that indicate that spirituality helps people cope with childhood trauma.[1]

> "Spirituality offers a way of coping when times are tough; finding meaning, connection and gratitude throughout our lives; and adding a rich and fulfilling dimension to our life."

It is worthwhile cultivating and grasping your own spirituality. Spirituality offers a way of coping when times are tough; finding meaning, connection, and gratitude throughout our lives; and adding a rich and fulfilling dimension to our life. When I stand and observe nature, I am transported to the awareness that I am a part of something so much bigger than my human mind will ever be able to grasp. I look at the trees swaying in the wind, and I think to myself, *I'm a human, and you are a tree. We each have our unique jobs to do here. We know pain, suffering, and loss and renewal, peace, and joy. We are together here, in this moment: both alive, sharing air and space, and a part of something big and vast.*

Spirituality—and how each of us finds it—is, of course, subjective. We all experience spirituality differently. I know many people who say they feel their most spiritual through connection to religious practice, and that is wonderful.

Others who identify as agnostic or atheist might find their spirituality in the trees and nature or their yoga practice. Some people find their connection to spirituality through their children—observing these miracles of life, watching their innocence, magic, and wonder can bring about intense feelings of spirituality. Others find spirituality through music, art, or poetry—either through creating or observing creations. These sorts of practices can really connect us both to ourselves and to the belief that we are part of something much greater and deeper than our little human forms grasp.

However you find it, it's worth finding.

Connecting with that awareness that this moment, this life, goes far deeper than your thoughts know, forms an important basis for doing the earlier work in this book: developing a loving relationship with yourself and allowing yourself to move into a more brave and grateful existence where you are not inhibiting your movement with thoughts of insufficiency and self-doubt but connecting with a much broader and deeper understanding of our place in all things. *Knowing* this, somewhere deep, deep inside of you, allows you to acknowledge and transcend the oft-held limitations of your mind and hopefully access your inner wellspring of wisdom and courage it takes to *be brave.*

Modeh Ani Lefanecha Melech Chai Vkayam

I have uttered this phrase throughout much of my life, first thing in the morning. These Hebrew words mean, "I give thanks before you, God, for you have returned within me my soul with compassion; abundant is your faithfulness!" I was taught to say these words first thing in the morning, to thank God for returning my soul so that I am able to experience another day.

Somewhere along the way, these words stopped holding meaning and became something I uttered by rote—part of the list of *practices* I felt encumbered by. Just as I was performing so many other childhood rituals, I repeated these words so I could check off the box to make God and other people happy and in turn feel good about myself.

To be honest, I don't know if they ever carried much meaning for me.

And then, from a rabbi at a class I attended, I heard a new interpretation that I loved. He said every morning when he recites this blessing, it is a moment of gratitude *and* mindfulness. These words create a pause that allow him to ground himself in his body and experience gratitude at being given another day. Not everyone is gifted one, and it is the privilege of innocence or denial that allows us to forget what a gift it is to wake up healthy enough to enjoy a brand-new day of possibility. Even on the hardest days, we are immensely lucky to be alive, but how often do we take the opportunity of a new day for granted?

Now for me these words are a moment of pause and mindfulness in which I am deeply grateful and aware of the blessing in being given another day. Reconnecting with this gem from my heritage is a conduit into appreciating the present moment—a way of setting up the day as being seen through the lens of gratitude.

As one of my mindfulness teachers, Jon Kabat-Zinn, put it, before you get out of bed in the morning, make sure you complete the process of waking up. At a retreat I went on with him, he recommended taking a few mindful breaths to ensure we are *fully* awake before waking up for the day. Now pausing with these words in the morning, or with my breath or body, are conduits for me to make sure I am really, truly *awake* for my day.

I was listening to a podcast interview with the Dalai Lama. He spoke of connecting, or *re*connecting, with the heritage and religious values into which you were born. He encouraged if you were a Christian to connect with your spiritual values of Christianity; if you were Buddhist, connect with Buddhism; and if you were Jewish, Judaism. I had never heard of a spiritual leader recognizing the validity of all religions and encouraging people to return to their roots, without inviting them to seek spiritual fulfillment elsewhere. These beautiful words resonated within me and sparked a yearning in me to reconnect with my rich Jewish heritage in a way that felt freeing and beautiful, not rigid and oppressive.

It is reconnecting to old values with a fresh perspective that can bring us so much fulfillment. This has been a long quest of mine: not to abandon the rich tradition from which I

"But I was missing out on something more profound by simply going through the motions."

came. For a long time, I kept up with religious observances *only* so that I could remain connected to a Jewish community and to pass these traditions on to my children. But I was missing out on something more profound by simply going through the motions.

Finding a different, fresher, and more intimate relationship with this morning prayer is freeing and connecting at the same time. And that's my quest—to feel as if I am alive and invigorated spiritually, in the tradition that I was born into.

Another practice I have come to with a new energy is the practice of lighting candles every Friday night to welcome the Sabbath. When I first began observing this custom after I was married, I would light the candles, sing songs, and relish the quiet time with my family. It was a beautiful practice for sure. It is something I have done every single Friday night since getting married years ago. Now, in addition to singing and looking forward to family time, I create moments after I light the candles for quiet, just for me. I stand, with my hands covering my eyes (as is the tradition), and pay attention to what I notice, inside and outside my body. I observe the love and blessings that surround me, and sometimes, the yearnings, hopes, and sorrows within me. Spending a moment of mindfulness at this time enriches the practice for me.

Each of us has experienced moments in life when we felt moved by a sense of something greater or deeper than our conscious awareness could grasp. Those are moments worth cultivating. No matter your own connection to religion or spirituality, you can tap into regular practices that bring a sense of awe and meaning in your life.

15

Inner Wisdom

The adventure of uncertainty.

Growing up, there was a big emphasis on seeking clarity to make decisions. When we had any decision to make, big or small, we would pray for clarity.

Now, at this stage in my life, you might say that I've developed something of a clarity aversion. For me, the word *clarity* rings the same as the word *certainty*. And certainty is something that doesn't really exist in this world. With just about everything, there is always going to be a small element of uncertainty involved.

I don't believe in clarity; I believe in *wisdom*.

The difference between the two terms is in the way I understand clarity: clarity holds a sense of linearity and certainty that is unrealistic and can even be harmful to our decisions. Barely anything we decide on will be black and white and totally clear. So many of our choices involve sorting through different shades of gray and ultimately embracing uncertainty and relying on ourselves that we have good judgment as well as the ability to deal with whatever consequences might arise from that choice.

> "Inner wisdom is something that we are all born with and is always within us—we just may have been trained out of noticing it, or have had things happen to us that make it confusing to identify."

Inner wisdom is something that we are all born with and is always within us—we just may have been trained out of noticing it, or have had things happen to us that make it confusing to identify. Inner wisdom calls on our ability to navigate between different options and use our judgment and intuition to discern between them. Whereas clarity reflects a sense of certainty that just isn't possible (and can easily turn into a thinking trap if we let it!), wisdom is something innate and a derivative of self-trust, an acknowledgment of the complexity of things.

We are all born with this swell of wisdom—you may even call it "intuition," or knowingness—but some way or another, we lose touch with it and forget that it is even there. Sometimes, past messages or trauma make it feel as if it is very hard to find our wisdom. Part of our journey in life is to reacquaint ourselves with our inner wisdom, the part of us that knows how to discern what it is we need, knows right from wrong, and knows that there is great beauty, hope, and depth in this world.

Part of doing this work is knowing when to work through (with a therapist) the parts of us that may be dealing with old trauma or pain that is leading us away from our wisdom or may be trauma or anxiety masking itself as wisdom.

It takes discernment to know when we need to seek help because we are having a hard time acquainting ourselves with our wisdom. Sometimes, asking trusted people in our life for their feedback can help point us in the right direction.

My practice with mindfulness meditation has led me back to my inner wisdom. Through meditation, I realized how much chatter was going on in my mind, and how constantly distracted and confused I was by all of it. Through the practice of mindfulness, which led to a cultivation of deeper self-awareness, I realized how my thoughts were acting as serious roadblocks that were preventing me from accessing my bravery, taking action, and making choices that were in line with my deepest dreams and desires. I learned to simultaneously notice the chatter and tap into my gut feeling to make choices that were aligned with my values. While I have made great strides, I know that this will be my life's work.

With this awareness, it is now up to me to make the choices and take the steps to do the things that I really want

> "If it's not a hell, yes!, then make it a hell, no!"

to be doing. And part of doing what we want to be doing means saying no to the things we really *don't* want to be doing. This frees up both the physical and mental space for the right opportunities. In short, if it's not a hell, yes!, then make it a hell, no! (and if it is a hell, yes!, well then, let's learn to invite it in with excitement and vigor, even if there is fear of uncertainty).

Several years ago, I was hit by how out of touch I was with my own inner wisdom. I was invited to help lead a women's trip to Israel. I was flattered, and at the time, I had trouble turning down opportunities. I also had a little baby, had recently started a new job, and had some philosophical differences with the trip leaders.

So what did I do? I hemmed and hawed, made several pros and cons lists, and postponed my decision, waiting for clarity.

I had a pivotal moment when I was talking with my mother-in-law about my trip dilemma, and she offered most quizzically, "But you don't want to go." It was so obvious to her that my gut was telling me this was not the right time or trip, yet my head was at the same time trying to persuade me why I should go (sometimes, other people in our lives can be great mirrors and help us see things we are having trouble seeing!). In that moment, I finally made up my mind, and shortly after called the leaders with my decision not to go—as hard as that was, because it went against a strongly ingrained behavior pattern.

It's not always about knowing what the right opportunities are; it's about learning to tune in to our inner wisdom to know what the wrong ones look like too. Take a pause right now and check in with yourself: what in your life gives you joy and meaning and energy? And what are you signed up for that drains you and isn't what you really want to be doing?

An exercise I learned at a mindfulness-based cognitive training I went to a few years ago can be really helpful in assessing how the ways we are spending our time are affecting us. In short, make a sample list of activities you do during the day, from the morning until you go to bed at night. So for example, you might write "wake up in the morning, check phone, take a shower, get coffee, wake up kids, make breakfast, take them to school, go to work, take a phone break," and so on. Next—and here's the interesting part—write the letter *n* next to the activities that are nourishing and a *d* next to the activities that are draining (some might have both letters). Is there anything you can tweak to increase more of the nurturing activities? Can you eliminate or tweak any of the draining ones? Did you find any you assumed were nurturing but, on reflection, find that they are actually draining? (When I first did this exercise, I found that much of my leisurely phone time was actually draining!)

Sometimes doing a concrete activity such as this can create time to reflect on how we are feeling in our lives and what pieces of our wisdom we might be ignoring.

Getting back in touch with my inner wisdom has been a journey. I've been learning to pay more and more attention to my gut instinct and wisdom and to notice and let go of much of the chatter in my mind. And this is a really important point: finding our inner wisdom and knowing must always be cushioned in self-compassion and gentleness. We don't want to beat ourselves up for not following our wisdom, or berate ourselves for having made choices that are not in line with our wisdom. That's bound to keep on happening for a while—we repeat the most wired and reinforced behaviors, and it takes time and patience and hard work to unlearn and rewire. So be patient with yourself, make slow and small changes, meet yourself with compassion for making mistakes or having moments when you know what you want but are having a hard time accessing the gutsiness it takes to do it.

Be kind. Be patient with yourself. After all, there is much wisdom in that.

"Be kind. Be patient with yourself. After all, there is much wisdom in that."

For a long time, I had a hard time making decisions because I was out of touch with what I actually wanted, and I valued other people's opinions of my life more than my own. So I didn't really flex the muscle of independent thinking (similar to the antishame muscle, perhaps).

One day, my best friend and her mother stumbled on nineteen-year-old me sitting high up in the bleachers of our local public high school, thinking, as they prepared to go for their walk around the track. This became a habit for me. When I was anxious, I would take my current journal out with me for a walk or a drive and write and make lists and try and solve all my problems.

Did this work and help me achieve clarity? Nope. I was actually overthinking myself far away from where my wisdom lived. This sort of overthinking can actually perpetuate feelings of depression and anxiety and doesn't resolve them.

"We need some productive thinking, lots of trusting and compassion, and some action to make change."

I have had so many clients with anxiety over the years who, upon learning a helpful idea or skill in therapy, enthusiastically told me, "Oh! I'm going to go home and think about that." In my more novice therapist years, I felt flattered that the idea resonated so well that my client would go home and devote more mental space to think about it. Now, when a client says that in session, we laugh together as I gently chide, "No more thinking! Just be with it. Let it settle in and get out of your head about it." Overthinking is an illusion; we think it will lead to more knowing or more clarity, but really, too much thinking is often a clue we are engaged in circular unhelpful thought and it usually keeps us stuck. Thinking about it may sound nice on paper but doesn't translate well to real-life changes. We need some productive thinking, lots of trusting and compassion, and some action to make change.

As I've gotten older, and participated in my own therapy over the years to help with my own discernment, I've learned to tune into my instinct, to understand what it is that I really want or need, without all the overthinking and unhelpful, perseverative list-making (sometimes making lists can be helpful, just not when it is done in a ruminative manner). Looking back now, I wish I had a mentor at the time telling me to stop the thinking and start the *being*, letting me know all this thinking was digging me into an even deeper hole and what I really needed was to learn to start paying attention to my wisdom to dig my way out of it.

Because I have a gut, and I have intuition; I had just lost touch with knowing what it was and, therefore, with listening to it.

And so do you. We all do.

We all have an inner sense of what we need, want, et cetera. We just need to listen to it.

This notion, this learning to tune inward, to hear ourselves, and trust it? It is huge, and it is unquantifiable.

It is also work to be comfortable with taking risks, being okay with uncertainty, and learning that often, *adventure* lives in that uncertainty.

16

Stepping into Who You Are

Standing up to shame.

The Roots of Shame

Many people grow up with some form of family chaos or stress. When we are younger, we often don't disclose our particular brand of family tension to others. When we are children, these realities can feel embarrassing to talk about, and we take responsibility for dynamics that were never ours to shoulder.

Every family is confronted with their share of stressors. Some more significant and challenging, and others less so. Still, many of us come out of childhood affected to one degree or another by what we witnessed growing up.

As I've mentioned throughout this book, there was high value placed on appearances in my community when I was growing up. Things at home were difficult, and yet to the outside world, I seemed to be thriving. I excelled at much of what I put my mind to, both academically and socially, all the while developing a good reputation. We lived in a big house in a new development. My father was a physician, and my mother was a music teacher. There were five of us children. I went to top schools. My life seemed uncomplicated.

And yet . . .

I didn't talk about the family tension: the financial stresses, fighting, and mental health struggles within the family.

I didn't tell anyone about these experiences, and I certainly never shared my yearning for a different, more open sort of life.

I fit myself into the mold I was being raised in, because I felt I *had* to.

It was survival.

In some primordial or subconscious sense, I think I knew that conforming and thriving was my ticket to succeeding and finding my own path.

And that's exactly what happened. Because I did so well in school, I got a full scholarship to a college I wouldn't have been able to go to otherwise, and this shaped my career path. If I had rebelled or not succeeded, I don't know what would have happened to me. And I thank God all the time for instilling in me the resilience and the wisdom to know, somewhere inside me, from the earliest age, how to adapt, survive, and succeed.

I never told anyone (with the exception of my husband and therapist) about my struggles at home as a child until my late twenties, when I had developed strong, mature friendships with women who could shoulder my old heaviness and share theirs. I pushed off so much of my personal development until I was older, because I didn't have the awareness of how I was being affected and it didn't feel emotionally safe for me to do so in my teens. If I had felt safe to share my struggles with others, I might have found the guidance I needed much earlier.

So why didn't I reach out, connect, and communicate with people who could have supported me?

Shame.

Going through personal tough stuff with my family paired with the shame-infused messages I received from the emphasis placed on appearances and looking "just so" was the perfect recipe for developing my own shame manuscript. Because things felt not "right" with me while my friends seemed to be doing just fine, I concluded there must be something seriously flawed with me. I felt that I was different than my friends—and not in a good way. Far from it.

As I've mentioned earlier, I grew up with strict laws surrounding how I was to dress my body. One of them was that I could only wear skirts that amply covered my knees, both when I was sitting and when I was standing. I remember being shamed for outfits I wanted to wear because the skirts were just at my knees and telling myself that I would be sure not to make that mistake again.

In my teenage brain, of course, I internalized the feeling that there was something wrong with me wanting to wear different kinds of clothes, shorter skirts or shirts with shorter sleeves. I can still remember those old feelings of embarrassment and the flush of my cheeks at that subtle shaming.

Shame is often used as a force to induce change in others. And the sad thing is, it often works. For humans, the feeling of shame can be debilitating and painful and is something many of us want to avoid at all costs. The threat of feeling shame or being shamed is enough to goad someone in a direction that is not truly reflective of who they are but of the desires of the other person.

Something I try to be very intentional about with my children is to not use shame as a way of getting compliance. I don't want my children to leave our home having internalized messages of comparison or there being something wrong with them. When we use comparisons as a method of change, it reinforces that who they are isn't good enough. There is implicit shaming happening when we compare one person to another in a negative way. In essence, we are saying: in order to be good, you need to be like so and so. It's much more effective to discipline our kids by focusing on them and talking about their actions without comparing them to others. I will sometimes notice the urge to use some sort of shame when disciplining my children. It can be tempting to say something like, "other people can hear you" or "other people are watching you" to stop a difficult behavior.

These words impart subtle shame and the message that we should make choices about how to conduct ourselves in the world based primarily on what other people think of us. As mentioned earlier, we want to move out of the human tendency to compare, and these messages of what other people will think of us feed directly into the comparison soundtrack.

There are other ways of correcting behavior and instilling values. There are ways of practicing emotional attunement in those hard-parenting moments and guiding our children to make a choice not because of what other people will think about them but because of who they want to be.

I want my children to believe that they are magic, *because they are.*

The wonderful thing about spending time with children is seeing their spark. They are a reminder to all of us that *we* were once magic. And we still are. It didn't go anywhere.

Many of the values I inherited from my youth were rooted in a desire to avoid judgment and shame.

Better not wear that color or that dress—what will people think?

I remember one time sitting in a bagel shop with some people close to me. My son, still a baby at the time, ripped off the beret I was wearing on my head. Everyone looked away, not directly acknowledging the incident and giggled uncomfortably, for it felt like great shame to be a married woman showing her hair in public. They felt embarrassed for me. They were ashamed for me.

I was ashamed, and I hadn't done anything wrong.

This was in the days when I still wore the traditional hair covering—still doing it, yes, but feeling silently resentful. It would still be a few years before I allowed myself to stop covering my hair. I remember telling them all defensively, "It's just my hair!"

To be perfectly honest with all of you, this old shame had a long shelf life. Even long after I modified my dress, it would pop up when I was leaving the gym in my workout clothes and bumped into the rabbi and his wife, who had known me in the days when I covered up my body. This happened often in the earlier days of my religious evolution. I learned to feel the shame, notice it, watch it, and allow it to float away instead of getting wrapped up and consumed by it. I reaffirmed that I am doing what is right for me, and I have nothing to be ashamed of.

But shame still pops up for me (albeit less frequently) and surprises me with its intensity. This is the power of shame, especially the shame that is born in childhood. I am thankful that today this shame experience is often coupled with a sense of gratitude and awe for my bravery.

> **"Because I *am* brave. We all are."**

Because I *am* brave. We all are. It was not that long ago that I felt okay with sending family photos to my family members who adhere to the strict religious laws I was raised with. For several years, I didn't want my husband to send pictures to my family that showed me in pants or with uncovered hair. When he would send pictures out to my family, I would get irrationally angry with him, because of the deep shame I felt from the worry of being judged. That's how stubborn our shame is—I think I am over it, and then, there it is: front and center and making me want to hide.

Our processing of shame reminds me of our human processing of grief, two powerful emotions. There is a lot written on how people process and work through grief. Elisabeth Kübler-Ross developed her well-known five stages of grief theory, which posits that as we grieve, we move through five different stages: denial, anger, bargaining, depression, and acceptance. We don't necessarily experience these different phases linearly and may bounce back and forth between them as part of the grieving process. I think this is similar to the experience of healing from shame. We may have done a lot of work processing our shame and feel as if we are no longer bothered by it only to find ourselves in a new situation that triggers a brand-new and powerful shame response.

A revered colleague of mine shared with me that she recently went to a special education conference—an area in which she has training and teaches. She was drawn to this work because of her own experience with a learning challenge. At the conference, which she helped organize, she was asked to wear a name tag identifying her as someone who lives with a learning challenge. She did it, openly and without reserve, because this is a part of her identity she has accepted, embraced, and openly tells people about. And yet, when she wore that tag, proclaiming her learning challenge, she felt shame, a surprising shame that was hard to explain and that she thought she had expunged long ago. And yet, there it was.

My family and I went on a trip over a holiday and took some beautiful photos. I didn't think much about what I was wearing until I was bit by the shame bug when I looked at some photos sent to my family where I was wearing a short-sleeved shirt.

Oops. And there it was, the shame.

The thing is, if we let shame drive us, we limit our lives to avoid the risk of ruffling feathers or making waves or falling short of other's expectations of us. It is the same with any self-limiting belief we might be encumbered with.

These old beliefs often stem from early outside influences. Messages from parents, siblings, friends, teachers—these are just some of the catalysts for deeply held shame.

And we need to watch that shame, the one that was planted while we were very little, because it is deeply internalized—but we can change how we respond to it.

When we suppress our feelings of shame, we unconsciously make choices that reinforce it.

> **"When we suppress our feelings of shame, we unconsciously make choices that reinforce it."**

This is like me not sending pictures to my family or veering off into another aisle at the supermarket when I spot someone who may judge me. (I've done this—on several occasions.)

Our shame is triggered, and we go into an automatic response of withdrawing and hiding, making ourselves small, because we feel so embarrassed, ashamed, of who we are, our essence. And then these behavioral responses unintentionally reinforce the shame belief that there is something inherently wrong about us.

But what if we stood up to shame? What if we quit letting it bully us and boss us around and tell us what to do or where to go? Why are we allowing shame to run our lives that way? It's like we're giving control of our lives to a nameless, fuzzy little (or big) monster—one that we build up in our minds but is really an illusion.

Instead, try this analogy that I often use in my therapy work: imagine the feeling of shame as a lovingly worn stuffed animal. Remember those days when you had lots of stuffed animals in your room? Some may have been quite tattered and worn, missing an eye or starting to tear at the seams, but it didn't matter at the time—they were cute and loveable. I used to have tea parties with *my* stuffed animals.

At nighttime, if the light is shining just right, that goofy, loveable stuffed animal can become a large, scary shadow on the wall. It is looming over us, and it causes us to cower in bed and feel worried. But all we have to do is turn the light on, and the shadow goes away; we see what the fuss was really all about: an old, tattered but loveable stuffed animal.

Shame functions the same way. When we don't face it—when we don't send pictures to our family because we are afraid of how they will view us—shame is the big and scary shadow on the wall. Yet all we need to do is face it, shed some light on it, and look it in the eyes, and it shrinks back to the small, unthreatening, and familiar old stuffed animal. Maybe even something that evokes a sense of deep compassion for our younger selves that learned to develop this response.

We need to look at our shame and face it over and over to learn to coexist with it peacefully and unencumbered.

That's what I tell myself when I go to my children's school pickup as one of the only mothers wearing pants (hello, fuchsia exercise pants). To flex my antishame muscle, I make myself *not* put on a skirt over my pants for pickup. Though I do admit, for a while there, there were times when shame overwhelmed me and I covered up. (We saved those bright-orange exercise pants for another time.)

> "We need to look at our shame and face it over and over to learn to coexist with it peacefully and unencumbered."

But seriously, in some ways it sometimes *does* get the better of me, and that is okay. Because I have developed the awareness to understand what is happening. I recognize the shame coursing through me, and I no longer feel controlled by it—most of the time.

And then? It passes.

So here's what I propose we do with our deeply held shame: Let's start looking at it, noticing it, being brave, and facing it. Talk about it; unleash it until we are bored of it. Remind yourself that there is absolutely nothing wrong with you and it is okay, it is good, to be different.

> "So here's what I propose we do with our deeply held shame: Let's start looking at it, noticing it, being brave, and facing it. Talk about it; unleash it until we are bored of it. Remind yourself that there is absolutely nothing wrong with you and it is okay, it is good, to be different."

And be forgiving of ourselves when doing this practice feels too tiresome, because that is an important part of acceptance, too (not to mention non-striving and compassion). We are not fighting it; we are not judging ourselves for having it—we are simply accepting it when it arises—and standing strong with our backs straight and our feet firmly planted on the ground. Nothing more, nothing less. Doing this will help us make different choices when shame pops up.

Take Up More Space

I learned a long time ago to fold myself up neatly into a square—like a nicely folded handkerchief. I was tightly folded, into a neat, safe bundle, and I trained myself that I didn't deserve—or need—more space than that. Taking up more space made me feel uncomfortable—it made me feel

> "Let's take up more space by talking more, asserting more, being bolder, and living a life that is most resonant with you. There is nothing shameful in that."

shameful. Let's unfold the corners of our handkerchiefs and lay ourselves out there, with all our truths. Let's take up more space by talking more, asserting more, being bolder, and living a life that is most resonant with you. There is nothing shameful in that.

Being a therapist for teenage girls has been an incredibly enlightening—and sometimes heartbreaking—experience. I cannot even tell you how many of these beautiful teenagers think they are ugly or fat or "not right." They feel shame every time they look in the mirror. I worked with a high school junior who for a period of about two years wore her hair so that it covered the "less attractive" part of her face. She could only see out of her one eye, friends, because her hair covered up the other one. And she was beautiful.

They all are. We all are.

I'm happy to say that, eventually, this young lady began wearing her hair away from her eye. At first, she would only do so at home, and eventually was able to display her precious face in all its glory, even wearing her hair in a ponytail so it was *really* out of her face. Her work in therapy centered on developing greater acceptance of herself and confidence in who she was.

Is your shame in how you feel about your body? Your children? Your marital or relationship status? Does it lie in your choice to stay home with your kids or your choice to go out and work and not be home with them? Let's just sit with that for a moment.

Can you let it go? Let the shame come up and then part ways with a little send-off. Put the stuffed animal on the shelf, or better yet, give it away. Thank it for serving its protective role in your life, notice a tenderness for the little you that was put in a position for the shame to flourish and allow it to float away. Give it a hug. And then, like a balloon, send it up into the sky, watching it get smaller and smaller. And then maybe look at yourself in the mirror, stare deeply into your own eyes, and remind yourself:

You. Are. Magic.

17

We Are Who We Are because of Where We've Been

It wasn't okay, and that's okay, and I'm okay.

Before we begin this chapter, I want to emphasize that experiencing past difficulties can be very painful and difficult to work through on your own. I am not talking about traumatic or abusive situations in this chapter. If you are dealing with old trauma or abuse, or old childhood wounds, seeking the support of a trained therapist can be very helpful in processing the pain of your past.

Our Parents Are Also Just People

I have to be honest.

It's possible I saved this chapter for last because it is the hardest one for me to write.

Not too long ago, I had an experience on a retreat looking at a photo of myself as a little girl, probably around three or four years old. This photo filled me with sadness over what little me experienced and what was to come, but I also noticed other feelings making the picture more complex. You see, I noticed that someone (probably my mother) took the time to cut my bangs in a straight line (no easy feat!) and was there, taking the picture of me. I was wearing a sparkly pink tutu, a costume I adored as a child (someone bought that for me!), and it reminded me of how much I loved to twirl and dance at that age. I was standing in front of our family piano (which now lives in my own house), which I loved to hear my mother play and myself would tinker over from a very young age. There was music and dance in my life too, amid sadness and loneliness.

I am often moved to tears when I think of where I've been, because I know, deep in my heart, that I wouldn't have the same level of resiliency had I not gone through those difficulties. I learned to be uniquely self-sufficient, to get to know how tough I am. To believe in myself and what I can accomplish. And now, as the adult woman that I am, *I* get to reparent the little me that was left lacking in some ways. I'm not sure if there is a purer way to live self-reliance and trust. Knowing that this sacred duty is on my shoulders now, to unconditionally love and support all the age variants of myself: me today and me from years and years ago.

In this way, gratitude can be an important partner for us when dealing with shame. We are not grateful *for* those difficult experiences, we are grateful to *ourselves* for our strength and resiliency in being able to *meet* difficulty, if not then, then now. We are grateful for being awake and alive to work through the muck and tough stuff, and for the ability to not be solely defined by it. We are comforted by the universalness in having pain be a part of life. It shows up for all of us, in some form or another, at some time or another. This is finding meaning in suffering.

Often when I am practicing gratitude, I thank God for my strength and ability to get through hard things.

In this same vein, practicing some cognitive flexibility may prove itself useful as well. This is to say, noticing the positive elements in how we grew up, what went *right* in our childhoods, or with the way we were parented, is a level of nuanced thinking that can lead to healing as well. Was there someone who helped you through tough times? When we allow ourselves to notice the good, the bad, and the ugly, in ourselves, in our parents, and in our past or current circumstances, we can get to a place of acceptance and, ultimately, healing.

> **"When we allow ourselves to notice the good, the bad, and the ugly, in ourselves, in our parents, and in our past or current circumstances, we can get to a place of acceptance and, ultimately, healing."**

This is something I've only been able to really appreciate as I've gotten older. Though my childhood was far from perfect, I am so deeply grateful for what my parents *were* able to give me. They came from their own difficulties, and the fact that they were able to love me, buy me food I liked to eat, take me shopping, host surprise birthday parties for me, help me edit my high school papers, and take care of me in many ways is profound. Becoming a parent myself has really helped me appreciate what I did receive and better understand the challenges of parenting.

There is so much power (and pain) in holding this duality: recognizing the suffering and loss in our own childhoods while being supremely grateful for what we *did* receive with the recognition that our parents were coming from hardship themselves. One does not have to come at the expense of the other, and opening ourselves up to this fullness is a practice of compassion for others, and for the self.

It's important to emphasize here that this isn't excusing poor parenting choices or saying we don't all need to take accountability for our actions. Or that we are giving parents a "free pass." Of course, in an ideal world, parents would process their baggage before having kids and not let it affect their children. However, this isn't the world we live in and isn't the story for so many of us. We take back our independence when we open to the perspective (and often painful reality) that we are all human, rarely are things all or nothing, and whatever hurt we endured was not personal.

For many of us, our parents are a large part of painful early experiences. Some of us had abusive parents—a complex situation that I'm not addressing directly here. But all of us will have to learn how to process the various ways our parents couldn't give us what we needed.

> "And so the cycle continues. Until it doesn't. Because you and me, we can be cycle breakers."

I believe part of this acceptance work is acknowledging the humanness of our parents. Just as we are struggling with a little person inside who was not met in some important ways within each of our parents who couldn't give us what we needed is another little person who didn't have their needs met in important ways. I know my parents underwent their share of early difficulties, leaving them with injuries that weren't addressed. And so the cycle continues. Until it doesn't. Because you and me, we can be cycle breakers.

This doesn't justify poor parenting choices; it helps with compassion and acceptance toward *ourselves*. Some of what we view as our parents' poor decisions are a result of their limited blueprint for how to be an emotionally connected parent or how to deal with emotions like anxiety and depression and rage.

They are human, just like you and just like me.

We are all imperfect. When we let go of the image of the all-powerful, all-knowledgeable beings our parents are to us when we are vulnerable children, dependent on them for our survival, then we can also let go of the identity of still being a victim, in our adult years. We may have been a victim as a child, but we can step into our power, process our pain, and learn to heal as an adult. We embrace our independence and our awareness that we can choose how we want to live our lives from this moment forward.

We can acknowledge we have been a victim in the past without being defined as a victim in the present. This is something we can move away from when we embrace acceptance and step into the power of being able to make our own choices from here on out (including finding a therapist to process your trauma if this is part of your story). We also learn to do this when we make behavior change or set and enforce our boundaries with people who continue to be sources of hurt and pain.

This also helps with letting go of the kind of bitterness that casts a shadow across our whole lives. Just like our parents are people, born out of their own stories and trauma, so are all other people, like misguided family members who are a product of the same culture. When we recognize the fallibility of all humans, it helps us be less bitter, because not one of those people was ever more of a human than you or me. They are not more powerful, stronger, or better. It simply may have felt that way as a child, but it is not accurate nor true. We can learn to stay with the feelings of deep sadness and loss (as is appropriate when there have been big childhood disappointments).

We are all equal in our humanity.

Just let that sink in for a minute, because it is a real game changer. We can and should mourn our losses, and the difficulties we experienced as a younger person. We can and should have boundaries so as not to perpetuate hurt or mistreatment. We can have hard conversations about our pasts with the people who have hurt us that may lead to healing and an embracing of your wholeness. And—this part is important—we can look with compassion at what happened to us honestly and allow ourselves to show up for that little person. But it doesn't have to define us by continued feelings of powerlessness.

We don't want to carry around resentment because that can be corrosive to our quality of life. When we are consumed by the bad things that have happened to us in the past, life becomes about those bad experiences and we completely lose track of the beauty of the present moments we have. The way I think about it is this: life was difficult before moments of change; then I took responsibility for my life and shifted things around. Why am I going to let the previous painful and sad moments continue to define and dictate how the rest of life will go? They are but one (formative and painful) chapter of my story.

But I can heal, and so can you. And that is another beautiful chapter(s) of the story: the chapter of healing. Here, I am the main character finding my power and making change. Learning how to live with loss in a way where it isn't following me around like an open wound, hindering my present or future. I can set the terms of my life—who gets to enter it, who I will have relationships with, and how I will honor and process my past difficulties. I want to be in those chapters.

It was difficult before; now let's make it awesome. We can do that you know. It all depends on taking control of our agency and how we define "awesome."

And how do we get to "awesome"? Well, the first step is by paying attention to what is already in front of you, in this very moment. Literally standing in awe and gratitude for this one life we get to live. The good, the bad, the ugly. The stuff we have control over and the stuff we don't. This one beautiful and complex—and beautiful because it is complex—life.

It Wasn't Okay, and That's Okay, and I'm Okay

We are all born with strength, drive, and wisdom.

Research supports that the many people who have gone through something traumatic grow from it. Several studies look at the mechanisms behind the growth that happens from experiencing childhood abuse. One interesting study hypothesizes that it is not the nature of the trauma but rather how the individual processes it and what they bring to the table that facilitates thriving.[1] We can choose to evaluate any situation in any number of ways. We have the ability of multiple perspectives for our own, and others', behaviors.[2]

Several years ago, I felt a strong pull from an inner wisdom that I needed to sit for meditation one morning. A family member had been going through a hard time, and on some level, it was bringing up old feelings of pain inside me.

So I sat with the intention to practice my basic sitting meditation. I was surprised by the flood of emotions that swelled over me. The little girl inside me needed attention, and it was she who was guiding me to sit. Tears flowed steadily from my eyes as the very old and thus familiar feelings of sadness and loneliness washed over me. And these words came to me:

It wasn't okay, and that's okay. And I'm okay.

This phrase offered me tremendous healing, allowing me to both validate and let go of old pain and reinforcing the acknowledgment that we have the power to make our lives what we want them to be. We don't have to be wedded to old pain or expired ideas of who we are.

I had spent many hours of therapy talking about my experiences, but this gentle and compassionate turning inward helped me take the next step in my healing. We can compassionately and generously take care of the little girl inside who didn't get what she needed and affirm that the adult version of ourselves, the current version of who we are, is okay. We are empowered, have wisdom inside, and have made brave choices. And will continue to do so, because that stuff—it ain't going anywhere.

Let's break it down.

It Wasn't Okay: Acknowledgment

Start with acknowledgment and self-empathy. No, it wasn't okay, whatever the difficulties you endured and were exposed to when you were a child. You shouldn't have had those messages thrown at you or those parts of you shut down. That's not the way it should have been, nor what you would have wished for yourself in an ideal world.

Spend a moment with that truth and allow yourself to feel the little you inside that was injured, to whatever degree you were—because most of us endured some sort of injury—and allow the tears to flow as you sit with this recognition that *it wasn't okay.*

And remember, as we mentioned earlier, acknowledging our painful feelings, without judgment, and letting them ride their course lead to greater well-being than avoiding them does.[3]

And That's Okay: Acceptance

Next, move to acceptance. It wasn't okay, but (and read this part carefully) it's okay to have had bad things happen to you (even if they never, ever should have happened—that's the duality here). It's okay to have had a less-than-perfect (even a far-less-than-perfect) upbringing. It's okay—it's acceptance—because we can't change the past. It wasn't ever okay or fair, and I will learn to accept what was because I will never be able to change it, as much as every fiber in my being wishes I could. We can't control much of what happens to us in life, however unfortunate or unfair. There is a lot of empathy behind these words. I can learn to let the past just be. Move away from the denial or the fighting what was. I can learn to finally set it down—lay it to rest. Honor it and process it and know we can't change what was.

The thing is fighting it, dwelling on the *should haves* and the *shouldn't haves*, is where the ultimate suffering lives, because we can't change the past. And fighting what happened to us is trying to change the past, which is impossible. Unless you have a DeLorean (with a flux capacitor), a

TARDIS, or some other time-traveling device, you simply cannot undo what has already been done.

When we try to fight our past—either by not wanting to recognize it and face it or by continuing to identify with it and getting stuck in the narrative of what happened—we become trapped in a rut. There is a certain peace that comes with true acceptance.

> *That bad stuff that happened and shaped some of my beliefs and took up years of my life never should have happened (it's not okay!). But it did, and here I am as an adult processing all of what happened. I am here to take back my power and part of doing that is knowing that I can't change the past. It's painful, and that's okay, because while pain is part of life, I am bigger than that pain, and I can't change the past, no matter what I do.*

Because, really, the empowered way of moving through tough stuff is a gentle and loving, real and honest, acceptance. There is great healing in acceptance.

And I'm Okay: Healing

The final step is healing. Try reading this paragraph out loud to yourself: I am whole. I am complete, just as I am, with all that I have been through. There is nothing missing inside me, I am not broken in any way. I am truly okay. I am okay with the hurt, with the old beliefs, with the old pain that pops up every now and then. I don't need any of that to go away to be okay. Because you know what? It never will. It will always be a part of me, my story, for my whole life. And my strength, and what I have chosen to do with my pain, makes me deeply proud.

The pain, the hurt, and the things that happened to us are like moss on a tree. The moss is covering the tree only superficially; it hasn't affected its body one bit. It is something the tree carries on its body, a marker of the passage of time and where it's been. The moss hasn't changed the gloriousness of the tree underneath one iota. In fact, it adds to the complexity of its story, pointing to historical depth. Your painful stories? Those are your tree's moss. They are something you carry, with respect and honor. They are markers of where you have been, but they haven't ever touched your core. Not even come close to it.

Where is your hurt? How are you holding on to it? How is it expressing itself in your life?

Holding on to old pain in a way where it is still open is, well, *painful*. It festers, eats away at us, distracts us from what is already before us, and drags us into the past, away from the present. We don't want to live in or from the past. We want to be fully awake for the present and all it has to offer.

Unfortunately, I know too many people who seem to be living from the past. They hold on tightly to unhelpful ways of seeing themselves, the world, and their relationships that they continue to feel powerless, even though they are adults and the hurt that was caused to them is far in their past. It can show up as an avoidance at looking at the pain or, on the other extreme, in an overidentification with it.

But the tricky thing is that life—is life. It happens—the good stuff, the bad stuff, the stuff that makes sense, and the stuff that makes no sense at all. If we wait on life, or blame life, or spend too much time and energy blaming the people who caused us early hurt, then we are letting go of so much of our power to create a life that is full and rich with meaning.

It is hard to see someone unable to step into their present and their future because they are sewn to their past. It is so sad because it is unnecessary; the key is already there, in that individual's hand, and they don't see it. It might feel easier in the moment to come back to the old pain, to use it as a reason for not moving forward in your life—it is safe, familiar, and, therefore, in some ways, comfortable. But we don't get any do-overs in life. This is it. Right here, right now. This is the only present moment you will ever get and be guaranteed to have.

Don't miss the beautiful moments you have access to every single day because you are immersed in the past.

You are okay. You are whole; you are beautiful. You are a complex human with a unique story. You have innate wisdom. You do. We all do.

You may have forgotten that over time or been trained out of seeing it, but it's there.

Conclusion

Recently, I was in my backyard watching the birds dance around and eat from a new bird feeder we put up. My attention caught a beautiful blue jay. It took a few steps forward toward the feeder, then retreated. Another few steps forward, and retreated. It came close to the feeder, but never made it all the way to get the food. I found myself rooting for it. "Go for it!," I thought. "You're nearly there! There is so much seed available for you. Don't let your fear make you fly away." The blue jay, for whatever reasons, did this dance a bit longer, and flew away. It didn't make it to the feeder that was so available for it, at least this time. There is a powerful metaphor here.

We started our journey reflecting on how we feel about ourselves, building ourselves up from our roots, and then moving into the more current and actionable lessons. We all have it in us already to live brave, full lives—we just may have lost touch with it somewhere along our journey's way. We all have difficulties, past and present. When we meet them in a way that is intentional and meant to propel us into a life that is rich, with meaning and with relationships—the ones you have with yourself, other people on this planet, and the world—well, it is exciting to think of what is possible.

We can and will overcome our obstacles; we will not let them define us or our experience of this life.

A few years ago, two people I have known almost my whole life commented to me on how happy I seem in my life. Now, my life is not without its challenges, but something about the implication of both these comments, together, hit me. It seemed that the intent was that my happiness in life right now was something of chance: "Wow, look at you, look at your life!"

I responded to both these people in the same way:

> "The way I am living my life is made up of a series of intentional choices."

The way I am living my life is made up of a series of intentional choices. Baby steps in the direction that aligns with my values. I have made a lot of active choices in my life to increase my well-being and joy. And many of those choices were hard. Gutsy. There are some days when I feel braver than others. And that's okay. I am human.

I know there is so much in life we have no control over. But there is also *so* much that we do have control over: our attitude, our individual responsibility to make daily choices that are in line with our own set of values and meaning, our sense of pride and satisfaction in making small and big choices that lead us down a value-driven path.

I chose to redefine my spirituality and bravely find a new system that works better for me.

I chose to connect with extracurriculars that fill me up and make me joyful and connect me with other awesome people.

I continue to choose how I will be with my body.

I stay connected to ideas and principles that I want to guide my life.

This means having the discipline to practice things I know are important to me. It also means connecting myself in a very concrete way to things that provide me with meaning, things like listening to a podcast on mindfulness (my favorite is Dan Harris's *Ten Percent Happier*), reading books and studies that further my knowledge of topics I am interested in, and so on. I also make sure to have an ongoing meditation practice, go on meditation retreats, and learn new mindfulness modalities that I can bring into my work.

When we practice our values in small, concrete ways, we build habits.

When we are connected to habits of well-being and personal meaning, we forge an identity that feels wholesome, *right.*

When we have an identity founded on things that feel purposeful and true to our souls, we access well-being and happiness and live fuller, truer lives.

When we face the hard stuff, take an honest look at it and learn to befriend it and allow it to coexist in our lives, we are brave.

Practicing bravery, gratitude, and self-care is the recipe for a deliciously alive life.

This choice—to live honestly, to live responsibly—is yours to make too. How will you move forward into your life, with this most awesome responsibility? How will you bring your own intentionality into your life to connect with it as deeply as you can? How will you—from this very moment and on—practice greater self-acceptance?

> **"Practicing bravery, gratitude, and self-care is the recipe for a deliciously alive life."**

The answers to these questions are all there inside of you, right now. Will you acknowledge them, place them as your guiding star?

Will you be brave?

Will you use your bravery to make gutsy choices?

You know what? You will.

You know how I know this?

Because you already have.

Acknowledgments

I would like to dedicate this book to my mother. With the passage of time, I am being reminded more and more of how short life really is, how we must cherish every moment we are gifted (even the hard ones), and how holding on to an accurate perspective in processing the hard things that happen in life is so important. My mother is a warrior; she is strong, and she is brave. She is definitely gutsy. She worked hard to raise five children coming from a difficult background herself. The fact that I always knew how loved I was (and still do, despite making different choices than what was set out for me) is profound.

I also want to dedicate this book to my eight-year-old self. Our inner children deserve and *get* to be celebrated, seen, and acknowledged. It is never too late, and we are never too old to turn toward our younger selves and give them what they needed but didn't get. I'd like to say to my little self, "I see you. I love you. You are a ray of light. Celebrate your uniqueness; don't ever feel like you need to stifle it. It is beautiful. It will lead you to a richly alive life. I've got you. You are stronger and braver and gutsier than you know. It's okay to have sadness be a part of your story. It makes you compassionate and caring and fiercely feeling. You are beautiful, and you can meditate with me any time you'd like. I'm here to sit with you, hold your hand, and hug you."

What would you like to say to your younger self? Maybe dedicate the changes you commit to making in your life to her. It's in her honor that from this moment forward, you live your life more bravely.

When we turn toward the sources of our pain, we can often find healing.

I also dedicate this book to all of you, dear readers, who are finding your way, dealing with difficult pasts or presents or both, who have yet to uncover all the fibers of bravery within you. My wish and blessing to you is that by the end of this book you start to know, with a resolution found in your kishkas (your insides), how brave you've been, are, and will be and how you can translate that into making real and remarkable change and shifts in your life. So much love to you.

I want to acknowledge my agent, Isabelle Bleeker, for championing my book and believing so strongly in the messages I felt called to share with the world. Your hard work, support, and accessibility made this whole process more fun and less overwhelming. The universe has an amazing way of bringing pieces and people together that we often don't get to see so clearly, but we are so blessed when we do. Thank you to the Broadleaf team, especially my editor, Lisa Kloskin, who was ever responsive and so helpful in her feedback.

Thank you to my amazing friends who have supported me throughout this endeavor, specifically Jodi, Deborah, Sara, and Emily, who spent the time to read early versions of my book and give me thoughtful feedback. With how busy we all are, giving your time to help me means so much.

I am so blessed that I get to be my children's mother (which I remind them of all the time). They are exquisite and unique. Their innocent curiosity and their ability to be more fully present in the moment, to be my best teachers in so many ways, to force me to confront shortcomings in myself, and to open the door for me to be able to reexperience life through the lens of a child inspire me every single day. And Yosef, when the weather is stormy, knowing I have you in my corner makes it more *sustainable*.

Notes

Introduction

1. D. Putnam, "Psychological Courage," *Philosophy, Psychiatry, and Psychology* 4 (1997): 1–11.
2. L. Grepmair et al., "Promoting Mindfulness in Psychotherapists in Training Influences the Treatment Results of Their Patients: A Randomized Double-Blind Controlled Study," *Psychotherapy and Psychosomatics* 76 (2007): 332–38.
3. Jon Kabat-Zinn, *Where You Go, There You Are: Mindfulness Meditation* (New York: Hachette, 1994).

Chapter 1

1. N. Zainal and M. Newman, "Relation between Cognitive and Behavioral Strategies and Future Change in Common Mental Health Problems across 18 Years," *Journal of Abnormal Psychology* 128, no. 4 (2019): 295–304.
2. J. Buhler et al., "A Closer Look at Life Goals across Adulthood: Applying a Developmental Perspective to Content, Dynamics, and Outcomes of Goal Importance and Goal Attainability," *European Journal of Personality* 33, no. 3 (2019): 359–84. https://doi.org/10.1002/per.2194.
3. J. Dickson, N. Moberly, and C. Huntley, "Rumination Selectively Mediates the Association between Actual-Ideal [But Not Actual-Ought] Self-Discrepancy and Anxious and Depressive Symptoms," *Personality and Individual Differences* 149 (2019): 94–99.
4. N. Moberly and J. Dickson, "Goal Conflict, Ambivalence and Psychological Distress: Concurrent and Longitudinal Relationships," *Personality and Individual Difference* 129 (2018): 38–42.

5. J. Laran, C. Janiszewski, and A. Salerno, "Exploring the Differences between Conscious and Unconscious Goal Pursuit," *Journal of Marketing Research* 53, no. 3 (2015): 442–58.

6. Virginia Tech, "Easy to Visualize Goal Is Powerful Motivator to Finish Race or Task," *ScienceDaily*, August 17, 2011, www.sciencedaily.com/releases/2011/08/110815143935.htm.

7. J. Silberman, "Mindfulness and the VIA Signature Strengths," *Positive Psychology News Daily*, March 27, 2007, https://www.wellcoach.com/memberships/images/Mindfulness &VIA1.pdf.

Chapter 2

1. S. H. Carson and E. J. Langer, "Mindfulness and Self-Acceptance," *Journal of Rational-Emotive and Cognitive Behavior Therapy* 24, no. 1 (2006): 29–43.

2. Carson and Langer, "Mindfulness and Self-Acceptance."

3. Brynne Demenichi et al., "Writing about Past Failures Attenuates Cortisol Responses and Sustained Attention Deficits Following Psychosocial Stress," *Frontiers in Behavioral Neuroscience* 12 (2018): 45.

4. E. Langer, Y. Steshenko, and B. Cummings, "Mistakes as a Mindful Cue" (unpublished manuscript, 2004).

5. J. White et al., "Frequent Social Comparisons and Destructive Emotions and Behaviors: The Dark Side of Social Comparison," *Journal of Adult Development* 13, no. 1 (2006): 36–44.

6. White et al., "Frequent Social Comparisons and Destructive Emotions and Behaviors."

7. P. Lockwood and Z. Kunda, "Superstars and Me: Predicting the Impact of Role Models on the Self," *Journal of Personality and Social Psychology* 73, no. 1 (1997): 91–103. https://doi.org/10.1037/0022-3514.73.1.91.

Chapter 3

1. Gordon L. Flett et al., "Dimensions of Perfectionism, Unconditional Self-Acceptance and Depression," *Journal of Rational-Emotive and Cognitive-Behavior Therapy* 21 (2003): 119–38.

2. Robin M. Kowalski and Annie McCord, "If I Knew Then What I Know Now: Advice to My Younger Self,"

The Journal of Social Psychology 160, no. 1 (2019): 1–20.
https://doi.org/10.1080/00224545.2019.1609401.

Chapter 4

1. B. Ford et al., "The Psychological Health Benefits of Accepting Negative Emotions and Thoughts: Laboratory, Diary, and Longitudinal Evidence," *Journal of Personality and Social Psychology* 115, no. 6 (2017): 1075–92.
2. K. M. Sheldon et al., "Personal Goals and Psychological Growth: Testing an Intervention to Enhance Goal Attainment and Personality Integration," *Journal of Personality* 70, no. 1 (2002): 5–31. https://doi.org/10.1111/1467-6494.00176.
3. I. Ivtzan, H. E. Gardner, and Z. Smailova, "Mindfulness Meditation and Curiosity: The Contributing Factors to Wellbeing and the Process of Closing the Self-Discrepancy Gap," *International Journal of Wellbeing* 1, no. 3 (2011): 316–26. https://doi.org/10.5502/ijw.v1i2.2.
4. E. L. B. Lykins and R. A. Baer, "Psychological Functioning in a Sample of Long-Term Practitioners of Mindfulness Meditation," *Journal of Cognitive Psychotherapy* 23, no. 3 (2009): 226–41. https://doi.org/10.1891/0889-8391.23.3.226.

Chapter 5

1. S. Côté and D. S. Moskowitz, "On the Dynamic Covariation between Interpersonal Behaviour and Affect: Prediction from Neuroticism, Extraversion, and Agreeableness," *Journal of Personality and Social Psychology* 75 (1998): 1032–46. https://doi.org/10.1037/0022-3514.75.4.1032.
2. L. C. Burpee and E. J. Langer, "Mindfulness and Marital Satisfaction," *Journal of Adult Development* 12 (2005): 43–51. https://doi.org/10.1007/s10804-005-1281-6.

Chapter 6

1. I think this is the right one . . . L. S. Blackwell, K. H. Trzesniewski, and C. S. Dweck, "Implicit Theories of Intelligence Predict Achievement across an Adolescent

Transition: A Longitudinal Study and an Intervention," *Child Development* 78, no. 1 (2007): 246–63. https://doi.org/10.1111/j.1467-8624.2007.00995.x.

2. Eve Ruddock and Samuel Leong, "'I Am Unmusical!': The Verdict of Self-Judgement," *International Journal of Music Education* 23 (2005): 9–22. https://doi.org/10.1177/0255761405050927.

Chapter 7

1. "Genetics vs. Genomics Fact Sheet," National Human Genome Institute, accessed October 1, 2021, https://www.genome.gov /about-genomics/fact-sheets/Genetics-vs-Genomics.

2. E. G. Thomas et al., "Gender Disparities in Invited Commentary Authorship in 2459 Medical Journals," *JAMA Network Open* 2, no. 10 (2019): e1913682.

3. G. Filardo, B. de Graca, and D. Sass, "Trends and Comparison of Female First Authorship in High Impact Medical Journals: Observational Study," *BMJ* 352 (2016): i847.

4. J. Protzko, C. Zedelius, and J. Schooler, "Rushing to Appear Virtuous: Time Pressure Increases Socially Desirable Responses," *Psychological Science* 30, no. 11 (2019): 1585–91.

Chapter 8

1. Tammy Scott et al., "Psychological Function, Iyengar Yoga, and Coherent Breathing: A Randomized Controlled Dosing Study," *Journal of Psychiatric Practice* 25 (2019): 437–50. https://doi.org/10.1097/PRA.0000000000000435.

2. M. Stork, C. Karageorghis, and K. Martin Ginis, "Let's Go: Psychological, Psychophysical, and Physiological Effects of Music during Sprint Interval Exercise," *Psychology of Sports and Exercise* 45 (2019): 101547. https://doi.org/10.1016 /j.psychsport.2019.101547.

3. J. R. Raibley, "Happiness Is Not Well-Being," *Journal of Happiness Studies* 13 (2012): 1105–129. https://doi.org/10.1007/s10902 -011-9309-z.

4. Thomas Curran and Andrew P. Hill, "Perfectionism Is Increasing, and That's Not Good News," *Harvard Business Review*, January 26, 2018, https://hbr.org/2018/01 /perfectionism-is-increasing-and-thats-not-good-news.

5. W. E. Davis et al., "Multidimensional Perfectionism and Perceptions of Potential Relationship Partners," *Personality and Individual Differences* 127 (2018): 31–38.

6. Thomas Curran and Andrew P. Hill, "Perfectionism Is Increasing, and That's Not Good News," *Harvard Business Review*, January 26, 2018, https://hbr.org/2018/01/perfectionism-is-increasing-and -thats-not-good-news.

Chapter 9

1. M. Feuille and K. Pargament, "Pain, Mindfulness, and Spirituality: A Randomized Controlled Trial Comparing Effects of Mindfulness and Relaxation on Pain-Related Outcomes in Migraineurs," *Journal of Health Psychology* 20, no. 8 (2015): 1090–106. https://doi.org/10.1177/1359105313508459.

2. J. Kabat-Zinn, "An Outpatient Program in Behavioral Medicine for Chronic Pain Patients Based on the Practice of Mindfulness Meditation: Theoretical Considerations and Preliminary Results," *General Hospital Psychiatry* 4, no. 1 (1982): 33–47. https://doi.org/10.1016/0163-8343(82)90026-3.

3. E. Garland et al., "Mindfulness-Oriented Recovery Enhancement Reduces Opioid Cravings among Individuals with Opioid Use Disorder and Chronic Pain in Medication Assisted Treatment," *Drug and Alcohol Dependence* 203 (2019): 61–65.

Chapter 10

1. W. Braud, "Experiencing Tears of Wonder Joy: Seeing with the Hearts Eye," *Journal of Transpersonal Psychology* 33, no. 2 (2001): 99–111.

2. P. Watkins, J. Uhder, and S. Pichinevsky, "Grateful Recounting Enhances Subjective Wellbeing: The Importance of Grateful Processing," *Journal of Positive Psychology* 10, no. 2 (2015): 91–98.

3. Philip Watkins et al., "Taking Care of Business? Grateful Processing of Unpleasant Memories," *Journal of Positive Psychology* 3 (2008): 87–99. https://doi.org/10.1080/17439760701760567.

4. K. O'Leary and S. Dockray, "The Effects of Two Novel Gratitude and Mindfulness Interventions on Wellbeing," *Journal of Alternative and Complementary Medicine* 21, no. 4 (2015): 243–45.

5. M. R. Hunter, B. W. Gillespie, and S. Y. Chen, "Urban Nature Experiences Reduce Stress in the Context of Daily Life Based

on Salivary Biomarkers," *Frontiers in Psychology* 10 (2019): 722. https://doi.org/10.3389/fpsyg.2019.00722.

6. K. Rankin, S. Andrews, and K. Sweeny, "Awe-full Uncertainty: Easing Discomfort during Waiting Periods," *Journal of Positive Psychology* 15, no. 3 (2020): 338–47.

7. Phuong Le et al., "When a Small Self Means Manageable Obstacles: Spontaneous Self-Distancing Predicts Divergent Effects of Awe during a Subsequent Performance Stressor," *Journal of Experimental Social Psychology* 80 (2018): 59–66. https://doi.org/10.1016/j.jesp.2018.07.010.

Chapter 11

1. E. Chan and S. Maglio, "Coffee Cues Elevate Arousal and Reduce Level of Contrual," *Consciousness and Cognition* 70 (2019): 57–69.

2. Jessica Rixom, Jessica Mas, and Brett Rixom, "Presentation Matters: The Effect of Wrapping Neatness on Gift Attitudes," *Journal of Consumer Psychology* 30 (2019): 329–38. https://doi.org/10.1002/jcpy.1140.

Chapter 12

1. S. Lin et al., "Social Network Structure Is Predictive of Health and Wellness," *PLoS One* 14, no. 6 (2019): e0217264.

2. Nancy Dess, "Tend and Befriend," *Psychology Today*, September 1, 2000, https://www.psychologytoday.com/us/articles/200009/tend-and-befriend. Quotes researcher Shelly Taylor, PhD, University of California. https://www.psychologytoday.com/us/articles/200009/tend-and-befriend

3. H. Klein et al., "When Goals Are Known: The Effects of Audience Relative Status on Goal Commitment and Performance," *Journal of Applied Psychology* 105, no. 4 (2020): 372–89.

4. Rick Kosterman et al., "Effects of Social Development Intervention in Childhood on Adult Life at Ages 30 to 39," *Prevention Science* 20 (2019): 986–95. https://doi.org/10.1007/s11121-019-01023-3.

Chapter 13

1. C. Chatzi et al., "Exercise-Induced Enhancement of Synaptic Function Triggered by the Inverse BAR Protein, Mtss1L," *eLife* 8 (2019): e45920. https://doi.org/10.7554/eLife.45920.

2. European Society of Cardiology, "Move More to Live Longer: Take the Stairs, Cycle to Work, or Exit the Metro a Station Early and Walk," *ScienceDaily*, April 12, 2019. www.sciencedaily.com /releases/2019/04/190412085238.htm.

3. Matthew Stork, Costas Karageorghis, and Kathleen Ginis, "Let's Go: Psychological, Psychophysical, and Physiological Effects of Music during Sprint Interval Exercise," *Psychology of Sport and Exercise* 45 (2019): 101547. https://doi.org/10.1016 /j.psychsport.2019.101547.

4. R. M. Ryan and E. L. Deci, *Self-Determination Theory: Basic Psychological Needs in Motivation, Development, and Wellness* (New York: Guilford Press, 2017).

5. M. Alda et al., "Zen Meditation, Length of Telomeres, and the Role of Experiential Avoidance and Compassion," *Mindfulness* 7 (2016): 651–59.

6. Anthony P. Zanesco et al., "Cognitive Aging and Long-Term Maintenance of Attentional Improvements Following Meditation Training," *Journal of Cognitive Enhancement* 2 (2018): 259–75. https://doi.org/10.1007/s41465-018-0068-1.

7. B. R. Gordon et al., "Association of Efficacy of Resistance Exercise Training with Depressive Symptoms: Meta-Analysis and Meta-Regression Analysis of Randomized Clinical Trials," *JAMA Psychiatry* 75, no. 6 (2018): 566–76. https://doi.org/10.1001 /jamapsychiatry.2018.0572.

8. A. Sommerlad et al., "Association of Social Contact with Dementia: 28-Year Follow-Up of the Whitehall II Cohort Study," *PLoS Medicine* 16, no. 8 (2019): e1002862.

9. F. Dominguez et al., "Association of Sleep Duration and Quality with Subclinical Atheroscleroisis," *Journal of the American College of Cardiology* 73, no. 2 (2019): 134–44; R. Avinun et al., "Reward-Related Ventral Striatum Activity Buffers against the Experience of Depressive Symptoms Associated with Sleep Disturbance 2017," *Journal of Neuroscience* 37, no. 40 (2017): 9724–29.

10. T. Huang and H. Redline, "Cross-Sectional and Prospective Association of Actigraphy-Assessed Sleep Regularity with Metabolic Abnormalities: The Multi-Ethnic Study of Atherosclerosis," *Diabetes Care* 42, no. 8 (2019): 1422–29.

11. Valley Health System. "How Much Sleep Do You Really Need, and What Happens When You Don't Get Enough?" *ScienceDaily*, March 1, 2016. www.sciencedaily.com/releases/2016/03 /160301175006.htm.

Chapter 14

1. Linda Skogrand et al., "The Process of Transcending a Traumatic Childhood," *Contemporary Family Therapy* 29 (2007): 253–70. https://doi.org/10.1007/s10591-007-9049-8.

Chapter 17

1. C. Woodward and S. Joseph, "Positive Change Processes and Post-traumatic Growth in People Who Have Experienced Childhood Abuse: Understanding Vehicles of Change," *Psychology and Psychotherapy* 76, Pt. 3 (2003): 267–83. https:/doi.org/10.1348/147608303322362497.
2. E. Langer, *On Becoming an Artist: Reinventing Yourself through Mindful Creativity* (New York: Ballantine Books, 2005).
3. B. Ford et al., "The Psychological Health Benefits of Accepting Negative Emotions and Thoughts: Laboratory, Diary, and Longitudinal Evidence," *Journal of Personality and Social Psychology* 115, no. 6 (2018): 1075–92.